The Treasure

Barbara initially trained as a music teacher, and worked as a music specialist in both primary and secondary schools. She has been in ministry in the Church of England for twenty-two years, first with the Church Army, and since 1990 as a deacon and then priest. Alongside NSM parish experience, she has held posts in prison, university and community mental health chaplaincies, and in theological education. Now working as a team chaplain in the Portsmouth hospitals, she continues to be involved in theological education at parish level, is a Continuing Ministerial Education tutor, and has been a local tutor for the STETS ordination course based at Salisbury. She has been involved in spirituality work in Portsmouth diocese for some years, and gives retreats, talks and workshops on prayer. Barbara is married to Martin and they live with their labrador Frodo in Emsworth, Hampshire.

Other devotional titles for Advent and Lent from the Canterbury Press:

Come Lord Jesus!
Daily Readings for Advent, Christmas and Epiphany

Geoffrey Rowell and Julien Chilcott-Monk

Stations of the Nativity
Devotions for Advent, Christmas and Epiphany

John Davies

Days of Grace
A forty-day journey with Jesus

Raymond Chapman

Flesh, Bone, Wood
Entering into the mysteries of the cross

Geoffrey Rowell and Julien Chilcott-Monk

The Treasures of Darkness

A spiritual companion for life's watching and waiting times

Barbara Mosse

Barbara Mosse

CANTERBURY
PRESS
Norwich

First published in 2003 by the Canterbury Press Norwich
(a publishing imprint of Hymns Ancient &
Modern Limited, a registered charity)
St Mary's Works, St Mary's Plain,
Norwich, Norfolk, NR3 3BH

www.scm-canterburypress.co.uk

British Library Cataloguing in Publication data

A catalogue record for this book is available
from the British Library

Scripture quotations are taken from the
New Revised Standard Version of the Bible
© 1989 by the Division of Christian Education of the
National Council of the Churches of Christ in the USA

ISBN 1-85311-542-8

Typeset by Regent Typesetting, London
Printed and bound by Bookmarque Ltd, Croydon, Surrey

To my husband Martin,

whose courage and compassion has taught me so much
about the treasures of darkness

Contents

Acknowledgements

I am very grateful to a number of people who have offered encouragement and advice in the preparation of this book. To the Rt Revd Dr Kenneth Stevenson for his warm encouragement, helpful advice and his writing of the Foreword; for those who read various parts of the manuscript and offered helpful comments and advice; Dr Paul and Mrs Barbara Bregazzi, The Revd Dr Roland Riem, the Revd Canon Alan Wilkinson, and the Revd David Gynes; to the Revd Dr Anthony Phillips for his valuable ideas on the book of Job. My thanks are also due for the encouragement I received from the Ven. Christopher Lowson, Archdeacon of Portsdown, who first urged me to explore these ideas further; my vicar, the Revd Robin Coutts, the Revd Andrew Tremlett, former Chaplain to the Bishop of Portsmouth, and the Revd Dr J. Philip Newell, former Warden of Spirituality for Portsmouth diocese.

Three groups of people in particular have helped me to put 'flesh on the bones' by allowing me to explore some of these ideas with them through prayer and meditation. For this I am indebted to the members of my Continuing Ministerial Education group in Portsmouth Diocese , and to two groups from the congregation of St John the Baptist, Purbrook, for their time, their openness and their willingness to share.

I would also like to thank four spiritual directors who have supported and guided me at different stages of my journey: the Revd Raymond Avent, the Revd Canon David Scott, the Revd Valerie Pearce and Alison Halliwell.

I am grateful to my editor at Canterbury Press, Christine Smith, for her wise advice and warm encouragement, particularly during those times when I doubted whether this project would ever be completed.

I owe the greatest debt of gratitude to my husband Martin, who read the entire manuscript and offered me the positive affirmation and constructive criticism that I so much needed as the work progressed. It is his constant love and support (and willingness to take on a larger than usual share of the housework!) that has made the writing of this book possible.

The publisher wishes to acknowledge with thanks permission to reproduce extracts from the following publications:

Euros Bowen, *Poems*, © Gomer Press, 1974. Used with permission from J. D. Lewis and Sons Ltd.

Jean Vanier, *The Broken Body*, © Darton, Longman & Todd Ltd, 1988.

Janet Morley, *All Desires Known*, © SPCK, 1992.

S. A. J. Bradley (ed. and tr.), *Anglo-Saxon Poetry*, © J. M. Dent, 1995. Used with permission from the Orion Publishing Group Ltd.

Common Worship: Services and Prayers for the Church of England, © The Archbishops' Council 2000.

Every effort has been made to trace copyright ownership of items in this book. The publisher would be grateful to be informed of any omissions.

Foreword

Many people repeatedly ask for help and nourishment in the seasons of Advent and Lent, because they can so easily be forgotten. There is always the rush to get straight to Bethlehem, and Lent has been so widely misunderstood in the past because so many people seem to associate it with giving up sugar in one's tea! In recent years, the Liturgical Commission of the Church of England have helped redress the balance, first with the book of services for Lent, Holy Week and Easter in 1986, and then the companion volume, *The Promise of His Glory*, for the seasons from Advent to Candlemas in 1992. But good liturgies still need to be backed up by the kind of devotional writing which reaches the hinterland of human experience, and that is precisely what Barbara Mosse has achieved in this perceptive and reflective little book.

Barbara brings a wealth of experience from her rich pastoral ministry, and this is reflected in the way that she relates the darker sides of human experience to the light of the gospel, whether it shines in the darkness of Advent hope, or the more pensive atmosphere of Lent and Holy Week.

So many people ask for books that will help them build a bridge between day-to-day experience and worship in the sanctuary.

The Treasures of Darkness will, I hope, meet that need for many.

+ Kenneth Stevenson
Bishop of Portsmouth

Preface

How to Use This Book

It is hoped that this book will be useful in a number of different ways. The initial inspiration came from a verse in Isaiah:

> I will give you the treasures of darkness
>   and riches hidden in secret places,
> so that you may know that it is I, the Lord,
>   the God of Israel, who call you by your name.
>
> *Isaiah 45.3*

This prompted meditation on other ways in which darkness is depicted as a source of riches in the biblical material. In time the scope widened and deepened, opening up into our own experiences of darkness as we travel through life. In the structuring of the material, acts and scenes suggested themselves, rather than sections and chapters. Our life cycle and experiences, and those of the people we read of in Scripture, are part of a cosmic drama which has its origins in the silence and darkness of pre-creation, and its fulfilment in the unimaginable light of the final consummation of all things. There are many acts and cycles within this drama, but these meditations began to find a natural focus around two of them; the experience of the Church's 'seasons of darkness' – Advent and Lent.

The book is therefore structured in two parts, based loosely around Advent and Lent – and can be used as resource material for those seasons. Each act has a slightly different flavour. Those aspects included under Advent tend to carry a general sense of darkness as an experience of waiting, anticipation and expectation, whereas those ideas explored in Lent bear a greater sense of darkness as a time of suffering, fear and questioning. But all of the topics contain a variety of nuances, and neither the Advent nor the Lent category is intended to be a closed system.

The first act consists of four scenes, one for each week of Advent. This leads us through some of the different aspects of the drama of waiting and expectation, as we look towards the coming of the cosmic Word of God in human flesh. In the second act, scenes for each week of Lent lead through a consideration of the darkness of pain, suffering and death which is a natural part of our human experience in the light of God.

But the material offered need not be confined to use during Advent and Lent. The treasures of darkness explored here suggest a rhythm and a pattern; a pattern conveyed to us – even in our age of advanced technology – through the timeless rhythms of nature; the sequence of the seasons, the inevitability of day and night, the ceaseless ebb and flow of the tide, the natural rhythms of our own bodies as we grow and age. Within this pattern we will have the opportunity to consider the experiences of renunciation, suffering and death in the lives of people who have found them to be the seedbeds of new life and hope, and to feel the resonance of such experiences within our own lives. As we begin to explore more deeply the implications of such experiences for our own journeys, we may well find it helpful – perhaps even advisable – to share aspects of our spiritual path with a spiritual guide or soul friend.

The resources section following each scene contains a diversity of material, and is intended to provide a flexible starting point for exploratory prayer-work by individuals or groups. Some suggestions for meditation are offered, and examples of prayer, poetry and prose writing from a wide variety of sources are included, in the hope of encouraging deeper exploration.

Above all, it is hoped that the material presented here will engage the reader with a sense of excitement and new discovery in prayer; as together we seek the God who calls us and reaches out to us through our experiences of darkness as well as of light.

Barbara Mosse
Advent, 2002

Act 1

Advent

Scene 1

Seasons of Darkness: Advent

I wait for the Lord, my soul waits,
and in his word I hope;
my soul waits for the Lord
more than those who watch for the morning,
more than those who watch for the morning.

Psalm 130.5–6

Advent sprang into vivid yet mysterious life for me some years ago, with a candle in the darkness of an early morning in a London winter. The symbols of the candle's light, the cold winter darkness and the season of Advent itself fused in such a way as to evoke a depth of hope and longing which was both difficult to articulate, and which I had never before experienced with such intensity. In the Church as well as in the world, the preciousness of Advent with its sense of hope and expectant waiting in the dark is often lost in the rush of pre-Christmas activities and preparations. In the season of Advent, we are invited to treasure its darkness, and to enter into the sense of yearning and anticipation it cradles. In the northern hemisphere the symbolism is rich, and Advent comes at the darkest and coldest time of the year when all creation seems dormant and lifeless. But as winter points inevitably to spring, so too does Advent darkness point to the coming of the Light of Christ at Christmas.

In her powerful Advent book *The Coming of God*[1] (to which I am indebted for many of the ideas in this chapter), Maria Boulding observes that the Church's season of Advent seems made for nature's season of winter, and we in the northern hemisphere have been blessed with the coincidence of religious and natural seasons and symbolism. I have always felt that the southern hemisphere has a much harder time of it, celebrating the seasons of Advent and Christmas in midsummer! Wherever we live in today's world, we attempt to manipulate the seasons through the use of artificial heat and light. We have cut ourselves off from the natural contact our ancestors had with the elements, the weather and the natural cycle of the seasons; we no longer really know what it is like to feel the wind on our face or the soil beneath our feet, and neither, since the coming of electric light, do we know what real darkness is like. There are very few places these days where one can go to find a depth of darkness which is untainted by even the faintest smudge of neon glow on the horizon. But despite our constant attempts to prolong our days artificially, stressing our bodies and our spirits by pushing them to ever-greater efforts against their natural and preferred rhythms, the season of Advent invites us, through allowing ourselves to really experience the winter darkness which accompanies it, to reconnect with something of the ancestral experience of darkness and long waiting for the coming of the light.

But there is an ambiguity here, and we will probably experience darkness as carrying a dual aspect. My experience of a candle in the early darkness of an Advent morning was rich, deeply moving and pregnant with mystery and promise in a way difficult to put into words. And yet as a child, I experienced – along with most children – a primeval fear of the dark which I felt to be a thing of terror and nightmare. As an adult on holiday abroad a number of years ago,

I found myself unexpectedly lost in the dark in a wood while trying to find my way back to the hotel. The darkness was so intense that I could not see my hand in front of my face. The fear I felt was terrifying and overwhelming, seeming to emerge from some primitive depth of which I consciously knew nothing. For our ancestors, lacking light and heat and with only limited food supply, the winter darkness would inevitably have been a time of fear and great peril. But today, we supposedly sophisticated inhabitants of the twenty-first century, may sometimes experience conditions and circumstances which strip away the sophisticated layers we have accrued, and we find ourselves starkly confronted with that which is most primitive and fearful within us.

So our feelings on engaging more deeply with Advent may be mixed; and we may feel, even while we complain, that the busyness of the pre-Christmas rush is somehow 'safer', and we can hide within it. But the tangible experience of darkness offers us an opportunity to connect hopefully with those experiences Maria Boulding calls the 'winters of the spirit'; experiences such as dryness, depression and loneliness; loss, pain and death, all of which will be explored more fully later in this book. We naturally shy away from grappling with feelings and experiences such as these, at least until we have to. But the message of Advent is that, however painful the experience, there is treasure in the darkness; that the darkness and dampness of the soil does indeed enfold and nurture the seed and its new life as it strives upwards towards the light. In Advent, God graciously offers us the gift of an experience of darkness under controlled conditions; for Christmas will follow Advent, as surely as spring follows winter.

In ancient times, the cultures of the peoples in the lands around the Mediterranean and further south came to see in the sun everything for which the people hoped and yearned: fertility, life in all its abundant fullness, and immortality. In Egypt and Greece, these longings found focus in the sun-god, who took the light away from the west each evening, travelled through the underworld during the night and reappeared in the east each morning, bringing the light with him. Roman peasants also worshipped the sun, and around the time of the beginning of the Christian era sun-symbolism had achieved a recognized place in the state religion of the Roman Empire. At about the time of the winter solstice, the Romans kept the Natalis Solis Invicti – the birthday feast of the Unconquered Sun. At this festival they celebrated the fact that the sun, at the time of its lowest ebb, began miraculously again to advance on the darkness.

It was in the fourth century that this Roman midwinter feast was adopted by Christianity, and the symbolism lent itself very easily to reinterpretation.[2] It became the feast of Christ's birth – Christmas – a time of dawning brightness from on high. People remembered Malachi's prophecy and saw in Christ the true Sun: 'But for you who revere my name the sun of righteousness shall rise, with healing in its wings' (Mal. 4.2). This interpretation was encouraged by the symbolism found in the biblical tradition, some aspects of which will be explored in later chapters. Israel, the people of promise, experienced both darkness and light through the successive crises of their history. The night of their captivity in Egypt gave way to the dawn of hope as they were led out to begin their journey to the Promised Land. In his book, *Ages in Chaos*,[3] Immanuel Velikovsky refers to the story of darkness in Egypt as related in the old Midrash books, which add supplementary detail to the biblical accounts. So thick was this darkness that no artificial means could dispel it; the light of any fire that was lit was either immediately extinguished by the ferocity of the accompanying storm, or else the density of the darkness was so great that it swallowed up the flame. On the Israelites' long march through the wilderness the nights were lit up by God who went before them as a pillar of fire, and the perception gradually grew of God as their only means of light:

> The Lord is my light and my salvation;
> whom shall I fear?
>
> *Psalm 27.1*

> Your word is a lamp to my feet
> and a light to my path.
>
> *Psalm 119.105*

In the depiction of the creation in Genesis, God calls light, life and abundant fruitfulness out of a dark, primeval and watery chaos. During Israel's experiences of exile the darkness took the form of loss: of their God-given homeland, of the temple which was the focus of their faith and belief, and consequently their cohesion and identity as a people. Through these nights of faith and experience, the Israelites lost everything they had thought was secure. They experienced the death of the God they thought they knew, only to discover him anew in ways which burst through the narrow categories in which they had previously confined him. As Isaiah had put it centuries before:

> The people who walked in darkness
> have seen a great light;
> Those who lived in a land of deep darkness –
> on them the light has shined.
>
> *Isaiah 9.2*

All Israel's prayer for help and their longing for salvation can be seen as a long watch through the night; of the night-watchman keeping vigil over the sleeping city, straining his eyes for the first signs of the coming of the dawn. The prophet Habakkuk sees himself as a watchman stationed on the ramparts, watching and waiting to see how God will answer him:

> I will stand at my watchpost,
> and station myself upon the rampart;
> I will keep watch to see what he will say to me,
> and what he will answer concerning my complaint.
>
> *Habakkuk 2.1*

The season that we have come to know as Advent seems to have had its origin in a period of December fasting in Rome; one of four periods of fasting during the year which were known as 'Ember days'. The original purpose of these times is shrouded in obscurity, although it is possible that they were established in the late fourth century in relation to the three pagan agricultural festivals. Certainly by the time of Leo the Great in the fifth century, Ember days were being associated with the seasons of the natural year. Significantly though, Leo saw the December fast, not as a preparation for Christ's coming, but as a thanksgiving for the past year's harvest. This theme of thanksgiving he linked with purification from sin, showing gratitude for God's providence through almsgiving, and the hopeful anticipation of the heavenly harvest at the end of the age. And although Leo does actually make use of the term 'Advent' at this stage, there is no suggestion that it is yet related to the feast of Christ's nativity; that connection had to await a later period of history.

During the sixth century we have the first intimation of

the December fast being seen as a preparatory time for
Christmas. It was longer than our present Advent – six
weeks instead of our four – and it began on the feast of
St Martin of Tours on 11 November. Appropriate biblical
readings were provided for the Sundays in this period, and
it is here that we have the first examples of readings directly
related to the nativity – the Annunciation (Luke 1.26–38)
and the visit of Mary to Elizabeth (Luke 1.39–56). With the
inclusion of other readings relating to the end of the world,
the signs of the times and the mission of John the Baptist,
the scene was set for the themes we recognize in the
Church's celebration of Advent today: preparation for the
birth of Christ, repentance and the coming of Christ in our
hearts, and the anticipation of his coming again at the end
of time.

Past, present and future; all are implicated in our experience
of Advent today, and we are encouraged and challenged to
embrace and explore each facet. The best of the traditional
Advent hymns encompass all three elements. The first
dimension of anticipation comes through our longing and
waiting for the birth of the Christ child at Bethlehem:

> O come, O come, Emmanuel,
> And ransom captive Israel,
> That mourns in lonely exile here,
> Until the Son of God appear.
>   Rejoice! Rejoice! Emmanuel
>   Shall come to thee, O Israel.
>
> > *Latin Advent Antiphons*
> > *trans. J. M. Neale*

Through the drama of the biblical narrative we can iden-
tify with the people of Israel, striving, falling and rising
again through the long night of their history as God leads
them through the darkness to the point of the dawn of
Christ's coming. For many of us, this yearning may also be
tightly interwoven with other personal memories: cold and
frosty mornings, the palpable stirrings of excitement in the
air, enticing 'Christmassy' smells emerging from the kitchen,
visits from much-loved friends and relatives, carol singing
in the cold night air, mysterious lumpy stockings at the foot
of the bed at the end of a long night's excited watch. But if
our memories of Decembers past are more clouded, less
joyful, then the message of the coming of the Christ child
proclaims release to the captives, and hope to the hopeless.
So Israel's past and our engagement with it; our own past
with all its memories; the light and the shadows, the joys
and the sorrows, our stumbling attempts to reach out and
embrace the love that God offers us so freely; all this can be
taken up and offered in the yearning, the hope and the
promise of Advent.

The second dimension of anticipation comes with our
longing for – and perhaps, our resistance to – the coming of
Christ, not just as a baby in a manger, but into our own
hearts and lives:

> O come, thou Dayspring, come and cheer
> Our spirits by thine Advent here;
> Disperse the gloomy clouds of night,
> And death's dark shadows put to flight.
>   Rejoice! Rejoice! Emmanuel
>   Shall come to thee, O Israel.

I heard recently of a church where a full-size stable scene had been built into the porch, so that people coming to the service literally had to go through the stable to get into the church. The reactions were mixed; some found it a powerful and moving experience, but others were heard to comment that it was far too realistic and made them feel uncomfortable. The danger of the Christmas-card depiction of the baby in the manger is that we sanitize it and try to make it safe; we armour ourselves against the blood, pain, sweat and filth that a human birth in such conditions must have involved. Simon Jenkins in his poem 'Babies' comments on the fuss we make over Christmas, which ends with the baby Jesus being safely put away for another year. If we 'put the baby Jesus away' at the end of the season we also shield ourselves from the need to listen to the words and accept the challenges of the grown-up Jesus, in his daily invitation to us to come to him, to put our trust in him, to commit our lives to him.

> Come, thou long-expected Jesus,
> Born to set thy people free;
> From our fears and sins release us;
> Let us find our rest in thee.

Charles Wesley

The third dimension of our Advent longing projects us into the unknown future, and the second coming of Christ in power and great glory at the end of time:

> Lo, he comes with clouds descending,
> Once for favoured sinners slain;
> Thousand, thousand saints attending

Swell the triumph of his train:
    Alleluia!
Christ appears on earth to reign.

Yea, Amen, let all adore thee,
High on thine eternal throne;
Saviour, take the power and glory,
Claim the kingdom as thine own:
    Allelluia!
Thou shalt reign, and thou alone.

Charles Wesley and John Cennick

Here we are projected forward, through the countless march of the centuries from the dawn of time and before, through and beyond the nativity in Bethlehem to that unknown and mysterious beyond-time when our God, through Christ, will reunite and reconcile all creation within himself. If we enter into the full invitation of Advent seriously, we will not be able to stay easily with the baby in the manger. The baby will grow up, inviting us to grow with him, urging us beyond the cocoons of selfishness and complacency with which we seek to protect ourselves; challenging us to nurture the seeds of the kingdom wherever we may find them, and to reveal the depths of God's love to a needy and alienated world.

Ideas for Prayer and Reflection

Almighty God,
give us grace to cast away the works of darkness
and to put on the armour of light,
now in the time of this mortal life,

in which your Son Jesus Christ came to us in great
   humility;
so that on the last day,
when he shall come again in his glorious majesty to
   judge the living and the dead,
we may rise to the life immortal;
through him who is alive and reigns with you,
in the unity of the Holy Spirit,
one God, now and for ever.
Amen.

Collect for the First Sunday of Advent, *Common Worship*

❦

Try to reconnect yourself imaginatively with your childhood
yearning for the coming of Christmas, or some other situation when you have experienced a yearning for fulfilment or
release. Try to remember and re-experience the growing
sense of excitement and anticipation, the intensity of expectation and yearning, the hope and promise of future
fulfilment. In prayer, imagine Jesus present in all of this,
consecrate your memories and feelings to him and welcome
him as the fulfilment of all your longing.

❦

Do not let our hearts incline to words or thoughts of evil,
but wound our souls with longing for you;
so that ever gazing on you and guided by the light that
   comes from you,
seeing you the unapproachable and everlasting light,
we may give unceasing thanks and confession
to you, the Father who is without beginning,

with your only-begotten Son,
and your all-holy, good and life-giving Spirit,
now and for ever, and to the ages of ages. Amen.

from the prayer of St Basil the Great, Orthodox

The grace which shone from your mouth
like a torch of flame
enlightened the whole earth;
it laid up for the world the treasures of freedom from
    avarice;
it showed us the height of humility.

from the Apolytikion of St John Chrysostom, Orthodox

Thus I saw and understood that our faith is our light in our
night: light which is God, our everlasting day.

Julian of Norwich, *Revelations of Divine Love*

Get up early enough to experience the darkness of a winter
morning. Light a candle and spend some time focusing on
the light shining in the darkness. Relax and deepen your
breathing, and silently repeat, 'You, Lord, are the source of
life; in your light, I see light.'

Sweet branch
From the stock of Jesse,
How magnificent
That God saw the girl's beauty,
Like an eagle,
Fixing its eye on the sun:

When the highest Father saw
The girl's radiance
And desired his Word
To take flesh in her.

For in the hidden mystery of God,
Her mind was filled with light,
And there emerged from the Virgin
A bright flower,
Wonderfully:

When the highest Father saw
The girl's radiance
And desired his Word
To take flesh in her.

Hildegard of Bingen, *Responsory for the Virgin*

O come, O come Emmanuel,
And ransom captive Israel,
That mourns in lonely exile here,
Until the Son of God appear.
    Rejoice! Rejoice! Emmanuel
    Shall come to thee, O Israel.

from a French Missal

Get up early enough to experience the darkness of a winter morning. Go for a walk outside, and take keen notice of your surroundings. Is the air cold and crisp? Damp and chill? Is there frost or snow beneath your feet, or the soggy dampness of the mouldering leaves of the dying year? Sense the dormancy of things; stay with the present moment and allow yourself to feel the difficulty in believing that new life and growth could ever emerge from this dank darkness. Then allow your mind and spirit to expand, reaching out for the promise, fulfilled year after year, that spring will come.

The prodigious expanses of time which preceded the first Christmas were not empty of Christ: they were imbued with the influx of his power. It was the ferment of his conception that stirred up the cosmic masses and directed the initial developments of the biosphere. It was the travail preceding his birth that accelerated the development of instinct and the birth of thought on the earth. Let us have done with the stupidity which makes a stumbling-block of the endless eras of expectancy imposed on us by Messiah; the fearful, anonymous labours of primitive man, the beauty fashioned through its age-long history by ancient Egypt, the anxious expectancies of Israel, the patient distilling of the attar of oriental wisdom by the Greeks: all these were needed before the Flower could blossom on the rod of Jesse and of all humanity. All these preparatory processes were cosmically and biologically necessary that Christ might set foot upon our human stage.

Pierre Teilhard de Chardin, *Hymn of the Universe*, 'Pensees'

Scene 2

Darkness: The Place of Revelation

Why art thou silent & invisible
Father of Jealousy
Why dost thou hide thyself in clouds
From every searching Eye

Why darkness & obscurity
In all thy words & laws . . .[1]

These words of William Blake give rise to some age-old questions, directed to a God who is often experienced as an enigma. Why does God so often seem to shroud himself in clouds and darkness? In the Exodus story and the book of Psalms in the Old Testament, darkness is seen, mysteriously, as the dwelling-place of God. At Mount Sinai, 'Moses drew near to the thick darkness where God was' (Exod. 20.21). In the book of Exodus and elsewhere in the Old Testament, the darkness that is experienced as God's dwelling place is seen in conjunction with the image of the cloud. 'He made darkness his covering around him; his canopy thick clouds dark with water' (Pss 18.11; 97.2). When Moses went up the mountain 'the cloud covered the mountain. The glory of the Lord settled on Mount Sinai and the cloud covered it for six days: on the seventh day [the Lord] called to Moses out of the cloud' (Exod. 24.15). 'Glory' is a rich term which encompasses great beauty and magnificence; wealth, substance and resplendent majesty. This glory is described as so overwhelming that it needs to be hidden from general view by the cloud. The cloud therefore serves two purposes; it signifies the presence of that which is awesome and holy, and at the same time acts as a protective barrier for those who are not yet ready to encounter the full holiness of God (Exod. 19.12). A similar experience is recorded when the Ark of the Covenant is placed in the temple in Jerusalem:

> When the priests came out of the holy place, a cloud filled the house of the Lord, so that the priests could not stand to minister because of the cloud; for the glory of the Lord filled the house of the Lord.

1 Kings 8.10–11

In the Exodus narratives, the cloud is a powerful symbol of the guiding presence of God in the wilderness:

> The Lord went in front of them in a pillar of cloud by day, to lead them along the way, and in a pillar of fire by night, to give them light, so that they might travel by day and by night. Neither the pillar of cloud by day nor the pillar of fire by night left its place in front of the people.

Exodus 13.21–2

The cloud, then, is a symbol of some paradox. Is it dark, like the darkness it sometimes accompanies (Ps. 18.11), or is it bright, shot through with the glory of God that it conceals? Is its purpose to hide – or to reveal? When leading the Israelites, we are told that 'the cloud was there with the darkness, and it lit up the night' (Exod. 14.20). We are perplexed by a collage of shifting images and perspectives; sometimes it is a dark cloud that is the symbol of God's presence, at other times the cloud lights up the night sky. The biblical language strains to express the inexpressible:

> If I say, 'Surely the darkness will cover me, and the light around me turn to night,' even the darkness is not dark to you; the night is as bright as the day, for darkness is as light to you.
>
> *Psalm 139.11–12*

It is clear that for the Israelite people the cloud was a visible sign of God's presence, in spite of the fact that his glory was hidden from them and only Moses was able to see God 'face to face' (Exod. 33.7–11). William Blake's poem at the head of this chapter asks many questions of this God who hides himself in clouds and darkness. We may well find this understandable; the idea of God dwelling in darkness may leave us feeling disturbed and uncomfortable. But for Moses and the Israelite people, the universal response to the mystery before them was one of worship and awe (Exod. 33.10).

The Old Testament symbols of cloud and darkness are rich and powerful. They signify to us that the God who created the universe and everything in it may be approached, loved and worshipped with awe and humility – but he can never be fully known in this life. The heart of God is light and love; but it is also mystery, and because of that mystery, his light and love will present itself to us as a kind of darkness – an 'unknowing'. A later chapter will explore this aspect more fully in relation to prayer and the mystical tradition of the Church. When talking of the first light of creation, that light which emerged in response to God's first command, 'Let there be . . .' the Celtic theologian John Scotus Eriugena referred to it as darkness, because it is essentially unknowable. This first light is not visible to our physical sight, although the clues of it are all around us. We can sense it in the beauty of sunlight dappling through leaves, or in the moonlight streaming across the water in an irridescent pathway; but these clues are not themselves the first light. They point beyond themselves to that which is invisible to our human sight – the 'Divine Dark'; or as T. S. Eliot in his 'Choruses from The Rock' calls it, 'Light Invisible'.

⸎

In our general experience, clouds are more accessible to our immediate senses. They are magical phenomena, replete with imaginative possibility. They form an almost continual part of our skyscape, ever shape-shifting, changing in form and function. A bright, cloud-bedecked sky may provoke a sense of wonder and provide food for the creative imagination, suggesting a fantasy country, complete with mountains and castles, coastline and ocean. As children, we would eagerly point out to each other the many animals we saw cavorting across the heavens; horses and dogs, a goat, and sometimes a fire-breathing dragon. And then there are the sunsets, with clouds streaked pink, purple and flaming orange. But clouds can also be dark and sinister, ominous with thunder and full of menace, foreshadowing the storm which is to come. Clouds are true vehicles of revelation, whether for the imaginative, creative mind, or as harbingers of the weather we can expect within the next few hours!

Although the New Testament does not describe darkness as the dwelling place of God in the same way as the Old Testament, the symbol of the cloud continues like a thread through the narratives, suggesting the mystery and the otherness of God. The cloud that descends on the mountain during the Transfiguration of Jesus overwhelms the disciples and fills them with fear. As was his frequent practice, Jesus had gone up a mountain to pray, on this occasion taking with him Peter, James and John. As he was praying, Jesus was transfigured before them; 'his face shone like the sun, and his clothes became dazzling white' (Matt. 17.2), and the disciples were given a glimpse of his glory. The location of the Transfiguration on the mountain resonates with the Old Testament narratives of Moses on Mount Sinai, encountering the holiness and majesty of God in cloud and darkness. In the Transfiguration, the resonances continue with the appearance of Moses and Elijah – representing the Law and the Prophets – as they talk with Jesus about his coming crucifixion – 'departure' in Luke's account (Luke 9.31) – in Jerusalem. The term 'departure' in this context means, quite literally, 'exodus', providing yet another clear link with the Moses experience. As Peter, overwhelmed by what he was witnessing, offered to build three booths for Jesus, Moses and Elijah, 'a bright cloud overshadowed them, and from the cloud a voice said, "This is my Son, the Beloved, with him I am well pleased; listen to him" ' (Matt. 17.5). In Matthew's account, the cloud and the voice had a similar effect on the disciples to that on the Israelites in Moses' time; they fell on their faces, prostrate with awe and wonder.

The cloud as a place of divine revelation is found through the whole sweep of biblical history. It is experienced as such in the Old Testament past, with Moses and the Israelites, in the New Testament present with the Transfiguration of Jesus, and it is projected forward into the apocalyptic future at the end of time. At the Ascension of Jesus it is a cloud which takes him out of the sight of the disciples (Acts 1.9), perpetuating the sense of mystery. As the disciples gaze after Jesus into heaven, they are told by two men in white robes that when Jesus returned, he would come in the same way that the disciples saw him go. Predictions of that time state that 'the tribes of the earth will mourn, and they will see the Son of Man coming on the clouds of heaven with power and great glory' (Matt. 24.30 and parallels). With the coming of the Son of Man at the end of time the revelation will be complete; the clouds will no longer conceal, they will reveal, and there will no longer be any room for doubt. 'Every eye will see him, even those who pierced him' (Rev. 1.7).

〰〰

In the experience of many people, 'darkness' may take a different form. During an interview, the profoundly deaf world-class percussionist Evelyn Glennie was asked how she would feel if she woke up one day and discovered that her hearing had been miraculously restored. Her thoughtful response was that, if she was able to have a choice, she would not choose to have her hearing back. Having become deaf during childhood, her other senses had heightened and developed through the years in conjunction with her musical ability. She had got to a point where she realized that, for her, not only was her 'auditory darkness' not a hindrance, it had become a positive and vital part of her musical and personal development. Her whole being had become intensely alive and sensitive to the minutest nuances of rhythm and beat, which she feared would be lost or at least thrown out of balance if her hearing were suddenly restored. Her experience over the years had been the discovery of a rich source of hidden treasure within the tragedy of her deafness.

It is today, sadly, still not unusual to hear of someone's struggle with an area of personal suffering being accounted for by an assumption that either they have sinned, or someone related to them has sinned; and that the personal darkness being experienced is some form of divine punishment. In the experience of the good man Job in the Old Testament, this was the line taken by his three so-called friends in their attempts to counsel him in the aftermath of the disasters that came upon him. Despite all appearances to the contrary, the friends' view was that Job must have sinned in the sight of God, in order to account for the catastrophe. For them, there could be no other explanation. When things go wrong today, the cry 'What have I done to deserve this?' is quite a familiar one; carrying with it the implicit belief that our way of life and the kind of people we think we are should somehow have earned us a better experience. Despite the fact that we know very well that 'the rain falls on the just and the unjust', there still remains an inbuilt human tendency to resent it when things do not go the way we would prefer. When Jesus encountered the man who had been born blind (John 9), the disciples, following the general beliefs of their day, concluded that the man's blindness was the result of incurring the divine displeasure. 'Rabbi, who sinned, this man or his parents, that he was born blind?' But this is a belief that Jesus does not share, as his reply makes clear. 'Neither this man nor his parents sinned; he was born blind so that God's works might be revealed in him.'

Jesus spread mud made with saliva on the man's eyes, and told him to go and wash in the pool of Siloam. The man obeyed and his sight was restored. As this healing took place on the sabbath day, it brought about an inevitable clash between Jesus and the Pharisees. The healed man was subjected to considerable pressure to state that Jesus was a sinner, but he stood his ground; claiming firstly that Jesus was a prophet (John 9.17), and later, that if Jesus were not from God, he could not have healed him (v. 33). For his pains and his honesty, the healed man was driven out of the synagogue. When Jesus heard of this he sought the man out, and led him on to a full confession of faith (v. 33–8). Jesus then stated that he had come into this world for judge-

ment, 'so that those who do not see may see, and those who
do see may become blind' (v. 39).

The miracle is an enigmatic piece, with shifting interplay
between darkness and light, blindness and sight, in both
the physical and spiritual dimensions. The man's physical
blindness was no barrier to his openness to receiving the
saving love of God, and as Jesus said at the outset, the
blindness itself became a vehicle through which the works
of God could be seen. The physical healing thus became a
visible symbol of the man's rebirth in the spiritual realm, as
his inner eyes were also opened. The Pharisees on the other
hand, convinced of their rightness and spiritual superiority,
were oblivious of the fact that they remained trapped in
their own inner blindness. 'If you were blind', said Jesus,
'you would not have sin. But now that you say, "We see",
your sin remains' (John 9.41).

A different symbolic use is made of darkness in John 3
where Nicodemus, a Pharisee and ruler of the Jews, came
to see Jesus 'by night' (v. 2). The negative aspect implied by
the use of a symbol of darkness here is one of spiritual
blindness and ignorance. Nicodemus wants to know how it
is possible for a person to be born again: 'How can anyone
be born after having grown old? Can one enter a second
time into the mother's womb and be born?' (v. 4). When
Jesus' explanation leaves Nicodemus more confused than
ever, Jesus responds, apparently with some exasperation,
'Are you a teacher of Israel, and yet you do not understand
these things?' (v. 10).

But unlike so many of Jesus' encounters with the
Pharisees, this meeting with Nicodemus is pregnant with
hope. Nicodemus is not proud, stubborn, or self-righteous.
A spiritual leader of the Jews he may be, but he senses that
there is more, much more to God than he has yet grasped.
He seeks enlightenment, so he reaches out in the darkness

to the light and revelation of Christ. We will explore Jesus'
encounter with Nicodemus more fully in the next chapter,
when we consider the idea of darkness as the womb of life.

❦

> I said to the man who stood at the gate of the year, 'Give
> me a light that I may tread safely into the unknown.' And
> he replied, 'Go out into the darkness and put your hand
> into the hand of God. That shall be to you better than
> light and safer than a known way!' So I went forth and
> finding the Hand of God, trod gladly into the night. And
> he led me towards the hills and the breaking of the day in
> the lone East.

These words, from a poem by Minnie Louise Haskins,
were spoken by King George VI as part of his Christmas
broadcast in 1939, during the dark early months of the
Second World War. The natural human tendency for each
one of us is to shun the darkness and reach for the light,
and indeed, to seek the darkness for its own sake could be
perverse and maybe even dangerous. But when darknesses
come upon us, as they inevitably will during the course of
every life, that is a different matter. It is then that we are
challenged to move through the pain and anguish that such
experiences bring, and to seek for the treasure hidden within.

A member of a small group, prayerfully meditating on
the idea of darkness as a place of revelation, found himself
picturing in his mind the paintings of L. S. Lowry, the
artist famous for his depictions of the northern industrial
landscape and its people. Initially puzzled as to why such
images had come into his mind at this particular point, he
then realized that one of the characteristics of these pictures
is that they were painted without shadows. This resulted
in 'matchstick men' and 'matchstick cats and dogs' (in the
words of a popular song of some years ago), making their

way across canvasses resplendent with light and colour, but no shadows or darkness. While imparting an immediate attractiveness and charm, this was nevertheless strikingly at odds with the sheer grinding poverty and misery which in the industrial north of the late nineteenth/early twentieth centuries was the lot of working class people, and which these pictures sought to portray. Light on its own is not sufficient; in art, shadow is also needed to suggest solidity, substance and form.

As in art, so also in life. We tend to imagine that we progress most when things are going well, whereas in reality the opposite is usually the case. When we are riding the crest of a wave we can become complacent, self-satisfied, and our awareness of our need of God can become blunted. The darknesses in our life often take us unawares, throwing us off balance and showing us how pitifully inadequate our own resources, apart from God, really are. It is in such experiences of darkness that we are encouraged to plumb the depths, and to discover the treasure within those depths that we never before suspected could be there. In the words of C. S. Lewis:

> Pain insists on being attended to. God whispers to us in our pleasures, speaks in our conscience, but shouts in our pains: it is His megaphone to rouse a deaf world.[2]

This chapter has been concerned with darkness as the place of revelation, and has used a number of scriptural and contemporary life examples as illustrations. It serves also as a fitting introduction to the chapters that follow because each one seeks to explore some of the ways in which this particular area of darkness may have the potential to become a place of revelation. In each one, with their different emphasis and focus, there is an underlying belief that this particular experience of darkness – whether it be dreams,

the Advent season, or some kind of personal suffering –
contains for us within its pain and questioning the potential
for a revelation of God's love and glory with an increased
depth and richness that we have not previously known.

Ideas for Prayer and Reflection

Almighty God,
who in the birth of thy Son
hast poured upon us the new light of thine incarnate Word
and revealed to us the fullness of thy love:
help us so to walk in his light and dwell in his love
that we may know the fullness of his joy;
who liveth and reigneth with thee,
in the unity of the Holy Spirit,
one God, now and forever.
Amen.

Collect for the Second Sunday of Christmas, *Common Worship*

An approach to meditation:

The frenetic pace of life that most of us live today does not
easily encourage a slower and more reflective way of being.
Through meditation, we are invited to slow down and listen
deeply to the God who is within us; to enter the stillness
with him who is ever-present in the heart of our being.

In the first instance, we will probably not find this easy.
We are so unaccustomed to living our lives in conscious
connection with God in the root of our being, that our early
attempts to do so may feel alien; a little like a form of darkness, in fact. But if we persevere, we will discover treasures
hidden and unsuspected; real, solid and life-transforming.

Begin by finding a place where you can be comfortable, and as free as possible from outward distractions. This may be a room, or simply the corner of a room, or maybe a place outside in the garden. Some people find the use of physical symbols helpful as a focus: a candle perhaps, or an icon, maybe a stone or shell, or some other natural object.

Find a comfortable position in which to begin your prayer. There are no fixed rules here; some find sitting on a relatively upright chair with feet flat on the floor helpful; others may prefer to walk, or lie flat on the floor. Whatever position you choose the aim is to be relaxed, yet alert, and it is probably best to have your back as straight as possible.

When you are ready, begin to repeat silently to yourself the verse found in Isaiah 45.3: 'I will give you the treasures of darkness, riches hidden in secret places.' You may find it helpful to time your repetition of the verse with the pattern of your breathing; 'I will give you the treasures of darkness' as you breathe in, 'riches hidden in secret places' as you breathe out. If you find this difficult, do not feel you have to force it; simply stay with the verse in the way which feels most natural to you. Know that as you do so, you are opening yourself up to the healing and transforming power of the God who dwells in the heart of your being.

Continue your silent repetition of the verse for fifteen minutes (again, there are no hard-and-fast rules here; you may prefer, if this way of praying is new to you, to begin with five minutes of silent meditation, gradually building the time up as you become more accustomed to it). As you meditate, you may find that various images, memories and ideas arise in your mind. This is nothing to worry about; simply acknowledge their presence, and then return to your silent repetition of the verse. Some people find it helpful to have a notebook to hand, so that thoughts that feel like distractions can be noted down and returned to later.

At the end of the fifteen minutes' meditation, sit for a few moments enjoying the silence, and allow the thoughts, desires and prayers of your heart to arise from deep within you. In the silence, offer all that comes to God, knowing that the deepest desires of your heart come from him and he is working deeply within you for your good. As a way of concluding your time of prayer and meditation, you may like to say the Lord's Prayer, or some other closing words.

If you have been praying alone, you may find it helpful to write down something of your feelings and experience in a journal. If you have been meditating with a group, a short time of sharing may be helpful to all.

♧

The love of one that makes distinction between the trials and the joys that he has of love cannot soar to the heavens.

Ramon Lull (c.1232–1315), The Tree of Love³

♧

Capo 3

I will give you the trea-sures of dark-ness, ri-ches hid-den in se-cret pla-ces so that you may know that it is I the Lord, the God of Is-ra-el, who call you by your name.

© Barbara Mosse, 2001

Scene 3

Darkness: The Womb of Life

Noye's Fludde, by Benjamin Britten, is an inspired musical setting of one of the Chester Miracle plays, arranged for performance by adults and children at the fourteenth Aldeburgh Festival in 1958. Britten skilfully incorporates the talents of all the musicians, from the most advanced players right down to the youngest beginners. The mounting storm and the consequent deluge are conjured up most graphically by the orchestra, building up from tiny beginnings to a shrieking cacophony of open violin strings and wailing woodwind. As the noise and the confusion reach fever pitch, and it seems as if all control of the orchestral forces – and the wild and unpredictable elements they represent – has been lost, the words and the music of the hymn, 'Eternal Father, strong to save', sung by the survivors in the ark, arise miraculously out of the chaos.

It is a stunning moment, and its powerfully moving impact remains with me over thirty years after I first heard it. The hymn, initially struggling to gain a foothold amidst the strident discord surrounding it, hangs grimly on, slowly gaining in power and growing in conviction. It acts like a magnet; slowly, but inevitably, it compels the instrumental forces towards it and away from their chaotic dissonance. Gradually the force of the storm diminishes, and by the end of the hymn all are united in a tremendous affirmation of faith and hope, arising from within the forces of chaos and darkness that had threatened to overwhelm and destroy.

The tempestuous chaos of the flood, so inimical to life, is an echo of that earlier, pre-creation chaos described so graphically at the beginning of the book of Genesis:

> In the beginning when God created the heavens and the earth, the earth was a formless void and darkness covered the face of the deep, while a wind from God swept over the face of the waters.
>
> *Genesis 1.1–2*

The 'wind from God' is sometimes translated as 'Spirit of God', and the verb 'swept' may also appear as 'hovered' or 'brooded'. The verb in the original Hebrew contains a suggestion of vibration, trembling and shaking which embodies a sense of urgent movement and involvement; an agitated stirring of an immense cosmic cocktail. 'Swept' would seem to capture with some effectiveness the sense of dynamic activity depicted here. The creative movement of God over this primeval darkness precedes his imperative declaration, 'Let there be light'; and that which appeared barren and devoid of any life potential issued forth in a teeming abundance of life in all its fruitfulness and fecundity.

We should not allow ourselves to be confused by the separation of the light of the first day of Creation and the creation of the heavenly lights – the sun and moon – on the fourth day. The light of the first day can be understood as 'the true light that enlightens everyone coming into the world', as the Prologue to St John's Gospel expresses it. This light is the necessary pre-condition for everything that follows; without it, nothing else would be capable of sustaining life:

Nothing has life apart from this light. It dapples through

the whole of creation. It is within the brilliance of the morning sun and the whiteness of the moon at night. It issues forth in all that grows from the ground and in the life that shines from the eyes of any living creature ... All life is rooted in the life of the 'first day'. In time God draws forth from that pool of light the countless streams of earth's life-forms and species ... The light of the first day is the source of our life and of all life.[1]

For the ninth-century Celtic theologian, John Scotus Eriugena, the account of the Creation in Genesis chapter 1 did not represent a fixed procession of creative actions which were completed over a number of days. Rather, it offered an opportunity to meditate on the profound mystery of creation which is ever-present, and ongoing until the consummation of all things at the end of time. For Eriugena all things – including ourselves – are part of that creative stream, and we have been hidden from the beginning in 'the secret folds of nature',[2] awaiting our time of physical birth. In other words, the Light of the first day is the source of all life that ever was, or is, or is yet to be.

This light, as we said earlier, is not to be confused with the visible lights of the sun and moon; it is of an altogether different order. Eriugena calls the light of the first day an invisible 'fiery power',[3] inaccessible to the human eye. As we sing in the words of one of our most well-known traditional hymns:

> Immortal, invisible, God only wise;
> In Light inaccessible, hid from our eyes.

And herein lies the paradox and the mystery; because if this Light of God is indeed invisible, inaccessible through our human senses, then inevitably it presents itself to us as darkness. The paradox is difficult for us to grasp, and we are fearful and shrink from it; we prefer the idea of visible light where all things are made plain. The nineteenth-century Celtic teacher Alexander Scott summed up our dilemma when he said the light of God in all things is not only 'bright', it is also 'awful'.[4] Just as the processes of human conception and birth are, despite our advances in scientific knowledge, still shrouded in an essential mystery and unknowing, so too much of the language used to grapple with the mystery of this creative darkness of God struggles to form itself in words expressive of procreation and birth. We have seen how the watery darkness of chaos, when seeded by the creative Word of God, gives birth to the earth and creation in all its myriad forms. The whole of the visible creation is shot through with the invisible light issuing from that Word, and were that light to be withdrawn, life would cease to exist. And yet its source remains to us a dark and unfathomable mystery, whose depths we are not capable of fully knowing. Eriugena summed this up when he stated that 'the Divine Dark excels every intellect',[5] a belief which also undergirds the *via negativa* (Negative Way) of the anonymous fourteenth-century author of *The Cloud of Unknowing*, of Meister Eckhart and the later mystic theology of St John of the Cross, to be explored in a later chapter.

❦

Another conjunction of the ideas of darkness, mystery and new birth is graphically portrayed in Psalm 139:

> For it was you who formed my inward parts;
>   you knit me together in my mother's womb.
> I praise you, for I am fearfully and wonderfully made.
>   Wonderful are your works . . .

My frame was not hidden from you,
when I was being made in secret,
   intricately woven in the depths of the earth.
Your eyes beheld my unformed substance.

Psalm 139.13–16

The human being is 'fearfully and wonderfully made', a mysterious and awesome work of creation made 'in secret, intricately woven in the depths of the earth'. In echoing the imagery of the secret growth of the seed, nourished in the darkness of the earth until it emerges to full maturity in the light, the biblical record affirms the kinship of the human being with all of creation. The Celtic tradition in every stage of its development has strongly affirmed this kinship, teaching that

> all life is interwoven, past and present, seen and unseen. Not only is the life of one species interdependent on the life of another, but the whole fabric of creation is woven through with the thread of God's light. It is like a material shot through with silk. If somehow this thread were removed the whole of creation would unravel.[6]

Celtic theology is only too well aware that sin and evil are an ever-present reality in our world, but believes firmly that their presence does not negate this thread of God's light. Whatever the magnitude of the evil, and however great its depth appears to be, the grace and the life and the light of God lies deeper still, awaiting its liberation. 'The light shines in the darkness, and the darkness did not overcome it' (John 1.5). The birth imagery used so effectively in Psalm 139 is found again in Paul's letter to the Romans. Here, the complex interweaving of the strands of light and dark, life and death, good and evil are brought together convincingly in the picture of the creation struggling to be born anew:

We know that the whole creation has been groaning in labour pains until now; and not only the creation, but we ourselves, who have the first fruits of the Spirit, groan inwardly while we wait for adoption, the redemption of our bodies.

Romans 8.22–3

The image of the whole of creation groaning in labour is a potent and dramatic one. There are echoes here of the creation account in Genesis chapter 1 where the Spirit/Wind of God sweeps over the face of the waters, and creation in its infinite variety of forms springs forth from the womb of chaos in obedience to the creative Word of God. The pre-creation chaos is depicted as a thing of darkness and ambiguity; so too are the labour pains of the new creation as it strives for birth into the full light and life of God. Darkness and struggle in this context involve pain, fear and uncertainty, but they also embrace hope, and the potential to become the womb of new life.

Jesus himself picks up the idea of darkness as the seedbed of new birth with his use of the image of the seed in a number of his parables about the kingdom of God:

The kingdom of God is as if someone would scatter seed on the ground, and would sleep and rise night and day, and the seed would sprout and grow, he does not know how. The earth produces of itself, first the stalk, then the head, then the full grain in the head. But when the grain is ripe, at once he goes in with his sickle, because the harvest has come.

Mark 4.26–9

With what can we compare the kingdom of God, or what parable will we use for it? It is like a mustard seed, which, when sown upon the ground, is the smallest of all the seeds on earth; yet when it is sown it grows up and becomes the greatest of all shrubs, and puts forth large branches, so that the birds of the air can make nests in its shade.

Mark 4.30–32

The process of germination and growth is shrouded in mystery, but without the dark enclosing of the earth, warmed by sun and moistened by rain, there would be neither growth nor harvest. The seed, dry, self-contained and apparently impervious to growth, needs to be buried in order for the miracle of new life to be brought forth. Jesus highlighted this paradoxical truth for his disciples when teaching them that, in order to grow in the life and love of God, they would find themselves having to die to self, and to opt for the darkness of self-denial and human misunderstanding:

Very truly, I tell you, unless a grain of wheat falls into the earth and dies, it remains but a single grain; but if it dies, it bears much fruit. Those who love their life lose it, and those who hate their life in this world will keep it for eternal life.

John 12.24–5

If they – and we – are able to yield in this way, then like the seed buried in the earth, the growth and the fruit that will result will be out of all proportion to the dark experiences which gave them birth. The new life that issues forth from this soil will provide enrichment and sustenance not only to each one who yields, but also through them to many others. They themselves will become life-bearers.

The biblical accounts of Christ's nativity indicate not only new birth emerging out of darkness as chaos, but also out of darkness as obscurity and unexpectedness. The choice of an ordinary young woman with nothing special to mark her out from her contemporaries and a humble carpenter to be the parents and guardians of Jesus, announce that this 'royal birth' is to be radically different from the expected norm. Even the conception, a mysterious and awe-inspiring process with any human being, is made even more mysterious by the overshadowing of the power of the Most High through the Holy Spirit (Luke 1.35). Thus the Holy Spirit who was active in the bringing of the first creation into being is similarly active in the bringing to birth of the new creation in Jesus Christ. The darkness of obscurity runs like a thread through the unfolding narratives. The parental couple live, not in Jerusalem where all Jewish hopes and longings were focused, but in the obscure and insignificant little Galilean town of Nazareth. The demands of the Roman census take Joseph and the heavily pregnant Mary to the town of Bethlehem, the city of David, because Joseph was descended from the house and family of David (Luke 2.4). Once there, crowded out of every inn in the town, the only place available for the birth is a stable shared with animals. News of the birth is announced, not to kings, emperors or religious leaders, but to a group of simple shepherds keeping watch over their flocks in the fields outside the town (Luke (2.8–16).

The symbolism of the night during which all these events are depicted as taking place is a potent one, and the darkness is seen as cloaking their true significance from all but a chosen (and unexpected) few. Sometimes, as in this beautiful nineteenth-century Celtic poem 'Christmas Carol' from the Hebridean collection, *Carmina Gadelica*, the darkness of night is compounded with the darkness of winter to provide

an even more powerful foil to the light of Christ which
bursts forth:

> This is the long night . . .
> It will snow and it will drift . . .
> White snow there will be till day . . .
> White moon there will be till morn . . .
> This night is the eve of the Great Nativity . . .
> This night is born Mary Virgin's Son . . .
> This night is born Jesus, Son of the King of glory . . .
> This night is born to us the root of our joy . . .
> This night gleamed the sun of the mountains high . . .
> This night gleamed sea and shore together . . .
> This night was born Christ the King of greatness . . .
> Ere it was heard that the Glory was come . . .
> Heard was the wave upon the strand . . .
> Ere 'twas heard that His foot had reached the earth . . .
> Heard was the song of the angels glorious . . .
> This night is the long night . . .
>
> Glowed to Him wood and tree,
> Glowed to Him mount and sea,
> Glowed to Him land and plain,
> When that his foot was come to earth.[7]

The symbolism of the night continues with the vivid
description of the journey of the wise men – the magi – from
the East, inexorably drawn on by the shining of a mysterious
star which they believe will lead them to a royal birth
(Matt. 2.1–12). As with the Hebridean poem quoted above,
T. S. Eliot's poem, 'The Journey of the Magi' underlines the
darkness imagery by compounding it with images of winter.
The wise men – although they may not have been kings as
the popular carol suggests – are nevertheless remarkable as

being the only people in the centre of the birth narratives who have any status in worldly terms. Herod, fearing for his own throne, seeks the child only in order to kill him; but the magi, also aware that they are in search of someone greater than themselves, seek only to worship. Their obedience to the call, cloaked and mysterious as it is, and their pilgrimage in a spirit of open-hearted searching, places them firmly in the company of Mary, Joseph, the shepherds, and all those who say yes to the God who veils himself in the obscure and unexpected.

❧❀❧

The imagery of darkness and night-time is crucial to the account of the meeting between Nicodemus and Jesus in John chapter 3. We are told that Nicodemus was a Pharisee and a leader of the Jews, and that he came to visit Jesus by night. The darkness here has a dual character which is both negative and positive. Negatively, the night-time imagery represents the darkness of ignorance, unbelief and growing hostility:

> And this is the judgement, that the light has come into the world, and people loved darkness rather than light because their deeds were evil.

> *John 3.19*

As a Pharisee, Nicodemus was a representative of that religious group who, along with the scribes, are portrayed in the Gospels as being the most hostile to Jesus, and the most deeply resistant to his message. But Nicodemus is different, as we see depicted in a graphic seventeenth-century poem, 'The Night' by Henry Vaughan:

> Wise Nicodemus saw such light
> As made him know his God by night.

Most blest believer he!
Who in that land of darkness and blind eyes
Thy long-expected healing wings could see,
When thou didst rise,
And what can never more be done
Did at midnight speak with the Sun![8]

There must also have been an element of fear and risk here for Nicodemus; to have approached Jesus with his questions in the full light of day could well have meant exposing himself to the judgemental suspicion of his peers. But Nicodemus was sincere and in earnest, and his quest was genuine. Unlike those apparently sincere Pharisees who asked Jesus questions simply in order to trap him, Nicodemus questions Jesus out of a genuine desire to learn and grow. As a result of his seeking, the darkness of night becomes, positively, a nurturing and protective environment, the womb containing undreamt-of possibilities of new birth and life (John 3.3–5). For Nicodemus, the leap of trust and faith involved in opening himself to the possibility of new birth will have felt pregnant with risk and promise. Risk, because he was being asked to relinquish all the old certainties and securities, and embark instead on something altogether less tame and predictable:

> Do not be astonished that I said to you, 'You must be born from above.' The wind blows where it chooses, and you hear the sound of it, but you do not know where it comes from or where it goes. So it is with everyone who is born of the Spirit.

John 3.7–8

With the parallel images of wind and Spirit, we are back at the beginning of Genesis, with the wind from God sweeping over the face of the waters at the beginning of the creation. The promise held out to Nicodemus is that all the possibilities of new life, beauty and creativity inherent in the wider creation will be available for the transformation of his life, if only he is able and willing to take that leap of imaginative faith and trust. And the darkness may well be the perfect environment for this:

> But living where the sun
> Doth all things wake, and where all mix and tire
> Themselves and others, I consent and run
> To every mire,
> And by this world's ill-guiding light,
> Err more than I can do by night.
>
> There is in God, some say,
> A deep, but dazzling darkness, as men here
>
> Say it is late and dusky, because
> They see not all clear.
> O for that night! where I in him
> Might live invisible and dim.[9]

Ideas for Prayer and Reflection

> God the Holy Spirit,
> You brood over the seething potential of our inner chaos
> with the brightness of your wings;
> transform our harsh dissonance into music for your glory,
> that we may live in your presence
> created, redeemed and renewed;
> through Jesus Christ our Lord.
> Amen.

Barbara Mosse

When we meditate, we connect ourselves more deeply with the God who is within us, the source of life and creativity.

Begin your time of meditation as before, in a place where you can be alone and undisturbed for a while. Commit yourself into the hands of God, opening yourself to his loving protection and the healing work he wishes to do within you. Take a few moments to find a position in which you can be comfortable and alert. Most of the time these days we carry tensions around in our muscles and our bodies without even being aware of it. One of the ways of dealing with this is slowly to tense and then relax each muscle group, beginning with your toes and feet, moving gradually up your body to the muscles of your neck, face and head. When you are relaxed, turn your attention to your breathing, making it consciously slower and deeper.

Begin to repeat silently the words from Psalm 139, 'The darkness is not dark to you; the darkness is as light.' As your meditation begins to deepen, you may find that memories or images of personal experiences of darkness in your life begin to surface. If so, simply acknowledge their presence, resisting the desire to bury them again. Offer them to God who is within you, asking him to reveal to you, in his time, the ways in which your particular experiences of darkness have the potential to become 'the womb of life'. Then return to your silent repetition of the verse.

After about fifteen minutes (or whatever time feels right for you), allow the focus of your meditation to turn outwards towards those you love, your local community, the whole created world and its people. Bring all that comes to your heart to God, seeking his light in the darkness. Bring your time of prayer and meditation to a close by saying the words of the Lord's Prayer, or some other appropriate closing words.

If you are praying as part of a group, you may find it helpful to spend some time in sharing something of your experience. But meditation is a very personal thing, so share only what you feel comfortable about sharing.

୧୬୫୬

God infused the seeds of every kind of life into man. Whatever seeds every one chooseth those spring up within him, and the fruits of those shall he bear and enjoy. If sensual things are chosen by him he shall become a beast, if reasonable a celestial creature; if intellectual an angel and a son of God; and if being content with the lot of no creatures, he withdraws himself into the centre of his own unity, he shall be one spirit with God, and dwell above all in the solitary darkness of his eternal Father.

Thomas Traherne[10]

୧୬୫୬

Scene 4

Darkness and Dreaming

'There is a dream dreaming us.'

Laurens van der Post[1]

'Could do better; she spends far too much of her time day-dreaming.' I lost count of the number of times I found that comment written on my school report. I did find it hard to understand this taboo on day-dreaming. Far from being a waste of time, day-dreams were for me exciting things; in them, aspirations took root, new directions and possibil-ities presented themselves, and creativity and imagination could take flight. For those who urged me to stick with 'reality', the darkness of day-dreams seemed to lie in their belief that they were a waste of time, diverting the attention from the more 'useful' and practical activities of everyday life. But for me, their darkness lay more in the area of mystery and pregnant possibility.

Whether we are aware of it or not, we all have an inner life; one which parallels, echoes, or compensates for the life we consciously live day by day. This shadow life manifests itself not only in imaginative day-dreaming, but also less consciously in the dreams we experience during our times of sleep. Dreams tend to mean different things to different people. Some consider them to mean relatively little; signify-ing no more than the brain's random method of dealing with the flotsam and jetsam thrown up by the events of the day. Some may claim not to dream at all. But for a countless number, stretching back through history to the dawn of time, dreams have been a surer key to reality than the merely conscious experience of the physical world in which they lived.

Dreams tended to be taken more seriously in the distant past, which seemed to be free of today's popular scepticism about their value. The Bible, both Old and New Testaments, is shot through with numerous examples. They are described in considerable detail; they are treated with great respect and there is generally a response to their message. In the Old Testament there are over 130 references to dreams and almost 100 to visions. There are a number of key examples in the New Testament surrounding the nativity of Christ, and during the early days of the developing Church, Peter asserts that the ancient prophecy of Joel is beginning to be fulfilled:

In the last days it will be, God declares,
that I will pour out my Spirit upon all flesh,
and your sons and your daughters shall prophesy,
and your young men shall see visions,
and your old men shall dream dreams.

Acts 2.17

Russ Parker[2] has calculated that the biblical dreams and visions, the stories surrounding them and the prophecies emerging from them, take up about one third of the Bible. That is a significant proportion, and gives some indication of the importance of dreams in the overall biblical perspective. Neither is this significance confined to biblical material; other ancient Near Eastern writings demonstrate similar interest. Dream libraries existed at Nineveh as early as

5000 BCE, and the oldest surviving work on the interpretation of dreams – from Egypt – categorizes the dreams according to whether they had a good or a bad effect on the sleeper.

One of the foundational beliefs of Christianity is that we have a God who not only loves us, but who also communicates with us in a variety of ways. Old and New Testaments demonstrate something of this variety; there is prophecy and the written word, the wonders of nature, acts of deliverance, and also dreams. The exciting thing about the idea of the dream as one of the vehicles of God's communication to us is that we all dream;[3] it is not just the privilege of the prophet, or the charismatic leader, or one who is judged to possess extraordinary faith or holiness. Certainly we read of the dreams of Jacob, of Daniel and of Jeremiah, and in the New Testament of Joseph and of Peter; but we are also told of the dreams of a sentry on duty (Judg. 7.13–15), a spoiled teenager (Gen. 37.5), and the worried wife of Pontius Pilate (Matt. 27.19). Dreaming is quite clearly considered to be an ordinary experience, offering us important information and a real potential resource for spiritual growth.

Visions and dreams are very closely related, but while dreams are a phenomenon of sleep, visions tend to occur when the subject is awake. J. H. Thayer in his *Greek–English Lexicon* gives the following definition of a vision:

> A sudden emotion whereby one is transported . . . out of himself, so that in this rapt condition, although awake, his mind is so drawn off from all surrounding objects and wholly fixed on things divine that he sees nothing but the forms and images lying within, and thinks that he perceives with his bodily eyes and ears realities shown to him by God.

However, just because the visionary may see things not normally accessible to the physical senses, it does not necessarily follow that the person's sense of reason and objectivity is overridden. This is made clear in Peter's response to the vision he receives in Acts 10, where the triple instruction to kill and eat the unclean animals let down in a sheet enables him to understand that 'God has no partiality' and that the gospel is indeed for the Gentiles as well as for the Jews. Peter's acceptance of the divine meaning of the vision enabled the gospel to begin to spread beyond the boundaries of the Jewish faith.

It was in the closing years of the nineteenth century and on into the twentieth century that there began to be serious attention given to the meaning of dreams. The first major work of real significance came from the Austrian psychiatrist Sigmund Freud, who firmly linked the process of dreaming to the activities of the unconscious mind during sleep. He was the first to establish that the sleeping mind was not in some sort of coma, but was, on the contrary, very much awake. For Freud, dreams related to events from both the immediate and distant past of the dreamer, and they represented attempts to come to terms with emotional and psychological tensions expressed in the individual's waking approach to life.

Freud did not believe in a transcendent God who may use dreams as vehicles of communication. For him, humanity was simply another species of animal with human decision and animal instinct being roughly equivalent. According to Freud, humanity's problem was not that it had lost touch with God, but that it had become divorced from the deepest parts of itself. Freud saw human behaviour as arising from three sources: the id, or unconscious, which is concerned with basic human drives and energies; the ego, which represents the conscious waking self as it interacts with its environment; and the superego, which represents the voice of authority, the moral demands of the community. Freud saw these three elements existing in an uneasy tension with one another, with the ego acting as the balance-keeper. Consequently, the threat from any potentially destructive forces would be repressed, or displaced through such means as jokes and dreams. So for Freud, the whole purpose of the dream was to give vent to those fears and fantasies that the individual and society as a whole would not find acceptable in waking life. The symbols of which the dream was composed were seen as disguising the real meaning of the dream, in order that the dreamer should not awake early because of fear. Many who came after Freud came to disagree strongly with this use of dream symbols, and to interpret them somewhat differently.

The Swiss psychiatrist Carl Jung was originally a friend and close disciple of Freud; but it was not long before he began to diverge from him over the approach to symbols in dream-interpretation. His principal point of disagreement was over Freud's insistence that dream-symbols were invariably sexual in their nature. For Jung, the symbols were altogether richer in their meanings and, far from intending to deceive, their purpose was to express meaning in much the same way that a plant reveals its blooms as it grows to maturity. Dreams, for Jung, were a compensation; they gave voice to feelings and emotions that were as yet unacknow-ledged by the dreamer; and they may serve as a warning as well as a statement of the dreamer's deepest desires. Jung claimed that the dream gave a true picture of the subjective state of the dreamer, a state which the conscious mind might struggle to recognize. The dream is quite straightforward, and pays no attention to the dreamer's conscious views on how things ought to be; it simply states how the matter stands.

I had reason to appreciate this a few years ago, at a time when Martin and I were planning to move house. We had looked at various properties in the area, and one day we went to see a delightful cottage on the outskirts of a village not far from where we now live. I came away from the viewing full of enthusiasm; the cottage was beautiful, and full of character; it had a long, sloping front garden running down to a small country lane, with an open view over fields and forest beyond. I was absolutely sure this was the place for us, and I took some persuading to listen to Martin who cautiously urged that we 'sleep on it' before putting in an offer. Sure enough, my dream that night told a very different tale. We were back at the cottage, but this time, the doorways were so narrow it was impossible to get inside. We were told we were welcome to buy, but there were not enough rooms and nowhere to put anything. I woke up knowing that my unthinking enthusiasm could have led us into a very big mistake. My waking self did have one or two reservations; all right, so the cottage was a bit small, but it did have possibilities. My dreaming self knew this was not the case, and told me so, firmly and unmistakably.

⟨❧⟩

A key element of Jung's philosophy is the concept of the shadow. We know that a shadow is created whenever light hits a physical object, and that the brighter the light, the darker the shadow that is thrown appears. Without the shadow, all the objects we perceive in our world would be flat and two-dimensional, a bit like figures in a painting by L. S. Lowry. It was Jung who first saw that there was a parallel to this phenomenon within the human personality; that there is a place deep within each of us where we store all those things we find painful, fearful, or which society has given us to understand are for some reason unacceptable. Freud may well have claimed that this was the same as his concept of the id, but Jung's theory transcends the narrow limits of Freud. Where Freud saw the contents and drives of the id as something primitive and dangerous, Jung saw the shadow as a place of hidden treasure. For Jung, the primary purpose of a person's life-journey was to work at, and hopefully achieve, individuation; that is, the integration of the contents of the shadow within the person's conscious life. Because just as a physical object is deprived of colour and vitality by the absence of a shadow, so is the human personality similarly depleted.

The poet Robert Bly[4] has described the personal shadow as 'the long bag we drag behind us'. This is how he describes its early development:

When we were one or two years old we had what we might visualize as a 360 degree personality. Energy radiated out from all parts of our body and all parts of our psyche. A child running is a living globe of energy. We had a ball of energy, all right; but one day we noticed our parents didn't like certain parts of that ball. They said things like, 'Can't you be still?' Or, 'It isn't nice to try and kill your brother.' Behind us we have an invisible bag, and the parts of us our parents don't like, we, to keep our parents' love, put in the bag . . . We spend our life until we're twenty deciding what parts of ourself to put into the bag, and we spend the rest of our lives trying to get those things out again.[5]

One of the things Bly warns against is the tendency to

idealize certain cultures; assuming that there are some cultures that have managed to avoid acquiring a 'shadow-bag' altogether. This is not so; the shadow inevitably accompanies the experience of being human:

> Different cultures fill the bag with different contents. In Christian culture, sexuality usually goes into the bag, and with it goes much spontaneity. Don't assume primitive cultures don't have a bag; it may be a different and possibly even larger bag. They may put individuality into it, or inventiveness. 'Communal mind' may sound positive, but it may simply mean that everyone thinks the same thing.[6]

Jung's belief was that, during the second part of life, the contents of a person's shadow increase the urgency of their demands for attention. Because while the shadow contains real treasure, its contents are not neutral; every part of our personality that we fail to befriend and absorb into our conscious selves will become hostile to us, warping our personalities and sapping our creative energy. Although pre-dating Jung and his shadow by some decades, Robert Louis Stevenson's novel, *The Strange Case of Dr Jekyll and Mr Hyde*, illustrates graphically the dangers of failing to integrate the contents of the shadow. Dr Jekyll is conscious that his nature is made up of light and dark elements, that he is a mixture of good and evil. He becomes fascinated by the different personalities these seem to represent, and discovers a drug that enables him to separate them at will. When wishing to give vent to his worst impulses he adopts the evil personality of Mr Hyde; a dose of the drug then restores him as the good Dr Jekyll when he wishes. As the story progresses however, the evil Mr Hyde gains in strength, and commits a horrible murder. Dr Jekyll also finds that he begins to transform into Mr Hyde involuntarily, and the drug no longer has the power to restore him to his original form and character. On the point of discovery and arrest for his crime, he takes his own life.

The contents of the unconscious need to be absorbed and integrated if they are not to become destructive for us. The paradox of this process is that absorbing the darkness of the shadow is not destructive, as we might first fear. What happens is that the energy spent in keeping the shadow aspects hidden and split off is brought into the light and becomes available for our use in a new and vital way. There are many ways in which we can engage with this process of discovery; but one of the principal tools available to each of us is our dreams.

❦

Jacob left Beer-sheba and went towards Haran. He came to a certain place and stayed there for the night, because the sun had set. Taking one of the stones of the place, he put it under his head and lay down in that place. And he dreamed that there was a ladder set up on the earth, the top of it reaching to heaven; and the angels of God were ascending and descending on it. And the Lord stood beside him and said, 'I am the Lord, the God of Abraham your father and the God of Isaac; the land on which you lie I will give to you and to your offspring; and your offspring shall be like the dust of the earth, and you shall spread abroad to the west and to the east and to the north and to the south; and all the families of the earth shall be blessed in you and in your offspring. Know that I am with you and will keep you wherever you go, and will bring you back to this land; for I will not leave you until I have done what I have promised you.' Then Jacob woke from his sleep and said, 'Surely the Lord is in this place – and I did not know it!' And he was afraid, and said, 'How awesome is this place! This is none other than the house of God, and this is the gate of heaven.'

Genesis 28.10–17

This dream, the first recorded in the Bible, is pivotal in the life experience of Jacob. His history up until this point has not had a great deal to commend it; cheating his elder twin brother Esau, first of all out of his birthright (Gen. 25.29–34), and subsequently out of his father Isaac's blessing (Gen. 27). At the moment when this dream occurs, Jacob is on his way to the house of his uncle Laban, in order to choose a wife from among Laban's daughters.

The dream is particularly significant on two levels, the religious and the psychological. On the religious level it represents a seismic shift not only for Jacob himself, but for the whole of Israelite society. Up until this point, the relationship between God and humanity had been a distinctly one-sided affair. The form it generally took was with an individual being addressed by a command of God, issued directly or through his intermediaries. The human recipient would have no say in the matter, and no automatic right of reply. The expectation was that the person so addressed would hear and obey – or the consequences could be drastic. But with Jacob's dream, the relationship was suddenly put on an entirely different footing:

The traffic of the spirit which had been so uncompromisingly from above to below, now was suddenly transformed into a two-way affair also possible from below to above. This would seem to be the meaning of the fact that in Jacob's dream the angels are both descending and ascending the ladder. The created is told, in the most authoritative manner, that he has an inbuilt system of communication for transmitting his needs to the creator and so receiving help in proportion to the will and purpose of creation inflicted on him. As the phrase would have it, for the first time a dialogue becomes possible between God and Man.[7]

Through the medium of a dream, Jacob sees, at a stroke, that the God who directed his life was a personal God. This is a God who promises Jacob – despite the wrongs in his past – that he will never leave him, and that he will keep his promises, to bring him back to the land and make of him a great nation. But this is no casual dismissal of the past, as if human misdemeanour did not matter. Jacob's life from this point on is to be far from easy, and there is a sense in which the gratuitous and utterly undeserved faithfulness of God conveyed through the dream confronts Jacob head-on with the sordidness of his earlier behaviour. He has not at this time come to a point of repentance, nor has he asked for help. Without such conscious awareness of need, Jacob is told that the creator God who is dreaming the future through him will always be there to support him from within. Such a relationship as is now being established requires not only gratitude and obedience, but also account-ability as a part of its response. Laurens van der Post comments that 'it is as if creator and created, through this dream, are being joined in an increasing act of partnership. Indeed, it seems as if the dream has taken charge of both God and man, and made them, however disparate the degree of their relationship, servants of a common purpose.'[8] Jacob responds to the dream with awe and gratitude. He names the place Bethel (House of God), and consecrates it by set-ting up his pillow-stone as a pillar, and pouring oil on it. He continues his journey with a new sense of God's purposes, and of his place within them.

༄༅༅

In the experience of some of the earliest peoples of our planet, among them the Bushmen of Africa and the Australian Aborigines, the dreaming process is enlarged and magnified to encompass the whole of the divine and created order:

> I was greatly moved when one of the first men of Africa, a Stone Age hunter . . . informed me, 'You know, there is a dream dreaming us.' To this day, I do not know anything to equal this feeling for what the dreaming process is to life, and the implication that it is enough for creation to appear to us as the dreaming of a great dream and the unravelling and living of its meaning.[9]

This idea of dreaming refers to the whole of life and the deciphering of its meaning. For the Aborigines, the Dreaming becomes a noun as well as a verb, encompassing the whole act of creation, the creator, the time of the creation, and the relationship between human beings and the other species. Because the time of creation is now as well as then, Dreaming becomes both a model for life, and a celebration of life as it is lived in the present. As a model, it acts as a kind of logos or guiding principle, conferring a quality of order and discipline. As a celebration, it glories in the living, dynamic abundance of life in all its variety and beauty of form. Dreaming is understood best when it is seen as a poetic key to reality, pointing to the eternal paradox of the creation with its discipline and order on the one hand, and its teeming, exuberant, ever-fruitful growth on the other.

To the Aboriginal mind, there is no aspect of the creation or its creator that Dreaming leaves untouched.

༄༅

> We are such stuff
> As dreams are made on; and our little life
> Is rounded with a sleep.
>
> The Tempest, Act IV, Scene I

In Shakespeare's late masterpiece, *The Tempest*, the world conjured up takes on a mysterious and dream-like quality. The island on which the drama evolves is the home of Prospero, the rightful but exiled Duke of Milan and his daughter Miranda. These two had been set adrift on the open sea twelve years previously by Prospero's usurping brother, Antonio. When Antonio and his companions sail close to the island, Prospero uses his magical powers to raise a storm and cause the ship to be wrecked upon the island.

What follows leads us into dream-like territory, where nothing is exactly as it seems. Calling on the services of the spirit Ariel and of Caliban, the mythical half-man, half-beast who was an earlier inhabitant of the island, Prospero uses a series of weird and wonderful theatrical devices to confront Antonio and his confederates with their guilt. The play-within-the-play adds further to the confusion and dis-orientation experienced on an island already full of noises and strange apparitions, and where the waking and sleep-ing states are strangely difficult to tell apart. Step by confus-ing step the shipwrecked royal party are led by Prospero's devices to a point of recognition, and they are able to accept some of the consequences of their behaviour. At the end of the play, Prospero releases Caliban and Ariel from his service, lays aside his magic, and prepares to return to Milan to resume his rightful dukedom. As everyone gets ready to leave the island, there is a real sense of waking from a dream, and returning to the real world of duties and responsibilities. But paralleling our own dreaming process, this has been a dream in which some measure of recognition, healing and restoration has taken place, and it is this which makes a return to waking life possible.

> Then Jacob woke from his sleep and said, 'Surely the Lord is in this place – and I did not know it!' And he was afraid, and said, 'How awesome is this place! This is none other than the house of God, and this is the gate of heaven.'
>
> *Genesis 28.16–17.*

Ideas for Prayer and Reflection

Almighty God,
you spoke to our forebears
through dreams and visions of the night,
bringing assurance of your presence,
warning of danger
and direction for the way ahead.
May we be open to your word in the sleeping hours of darkness,
and alive to your presence with our dreaming self;
that restored and refreshed,
we may with confidence greet the new day's dawn,
through Jesus Christ our Lord,
Amen.

Barbara Mosse

Believing as I do that the dream is not a waste product of the mind expelled through some sewage system of the spirit but a manifestation of first and abiding meaning, I thought I should enlarge St John's theme to include the idea that in the beginning there was a dream. This dream was with God and indeed was God. Somehow this dream demanded that it should be lived. As St John might have put it, 'the dream was made flesh'.

Laurens van der Post[10]

❧

Now the birth of Jesus the Messiah took place in this way. When his mother Mary had been engaged to Joseph, but before they lived together, she was found to be with child from the Holy Spirit. Her husband Joseph, being a righteous man and unwilling to expose her to public disgrace, planned to dismiss her quietly. But just when he had resolved to do this, an angel of the Lord appeared to him in a dream and said, 'Joseph, son of David, do not be afraid to take Mary as your wife, for the child conceived in her is from the Holy Spirit. She will bear a son, and you are to name him Jesus, for he will save his people from their sins. All this took place to fulfill what had been spoken by the Lord through the prophet:

> "Look, the virgin shall conceive
> and bear a son,
> and they shall name him
> Emmanuel",

which means, "God is with us."' When Joseph awoke from sleep, he did what the angel of the Lord commanded him.

Matthew 1.18–24

❧

Consider the possibility that your dreams may be one channel of communication between God and you. As you settle
down to sleep, commit your sleeping self into God's hands,
and ask that he would alert your unconscious mind to his
purposes and direction. You may find it helpful to record
your dreams in a journal, and to share some of your experiences with a spiritual director/soul friend.

❦

When you are faced with a seemingly intractable problem,
or you have to deliver a talk or a sermon that isn't coming
easily, try, literally, to 'sleep on it'. Commit the problem to
God before you sleep, and you may find when you wake
that the way forward has become much clearer.

❦

When [the wise men] saw that the star had stopped, they
were overwhelmed with joy. On entering the house, they
saw the child with Mary his mother; and they knelt down
and paid him homage. Then, opening their treasure
chests, they offered him gifts of gold, frankincense, and
myrrh. And having been warned in a dream not to return
to Herod, they left for their own country by another
road.

Matthew 2.10–12

❦

Heavenly Father, I thank you that waking or sleeping,
you are the God of my salvation. Father, I come to you
for more healing and invite you to show me more of
myself as you desire. I give to you my sleep for this night
and ask that, through Jesus Christ my Lord, you will

grant me to know more truth through my dreams; and that by listening to them I shall be free to serve you more, through Jesus Christ my Lord. Amen.

Russ Parker

Act 2

Lent

Scene 1

Seasons of Darkness: Lent

Forty days and forty nights
Thou wast fasting in the wild;
Forty days and forty nights
Tempted, and yet undefiled . . .

Shall not we thy sorrows share,
And from earthly joys abstain,
Fasting with unceasing prayer,
Glad with thee to suffer pain?

G. H. Smyttan and Francis Pott

The potent symbol of the wilderness has a long history in
both Christian and pre-Christian religious experience. It
was God's chosen testing-ground for the Israelites after
their miraculous deliverance from Egypt; the place where
they were born as a nation and took their first halting steps
in response to the God who loved them and was leading
them ever onward. It was in their long forty years' wander-
ing in the wilderness that through rebellion and repentance,
they slowly began to grow in obedience and trust. The
people frequently grumbled and complained, saying that
the fleshpots of their captivity in Egypt were preferable to
this so-called freedom in the wilderness, where they did not
know where their next meal was coming from. But despite

the setbacks, doubts and struggles, it was here that they began to discern the mysterious presence of God, feeding them with heavenly manna and leading them with the pillars of fire and cloud.

❦

Jesus' forty days in the wilderness at the beginning of his public ministry (Matt. 4.1–11) is in some senses a mirror to the Israelites' forty-year wilderness experience. Although, unlike the Israelites, Jesus was not leaving the 'fleshpots' or captivity of his former life, the experience nevertheless was one of deep challenge and temptation, through which his purpose and direction were clarified. The Church's celebration of Lent has been associated for so long with this time in the wilderness, that it comes as something of a surprise to discover that this has not always been the case. A direct link only came to be made early in the fourth century,[1] when Bishop Peter, Patriarch of Alexandria, enjoined a forty-day fast for penitent apostates who wished to return to the faith after denying it under persecution. The development of the Lenten traditions during the earliest centuries were complex and varied in detail between one area and another, but in broad outline the common understanding was that the season served as a period of intense final preparation for those who were seeking baptism at Easter.

As the Church developed from persecuted sect to acknowledged state religion, full acceptance brought its own set of problems. When no longer having to fight for its life, and when official acceptance has perhaps blunted the urgency of the message, the danger is that the Church will lose that vital sense of connection and immediacy. When the memory of the original events has grown dim, and the eyewitnesses to those original events have died, how is the foundational inspiration and motivation to be kept alive? Throughout its history, the Church has developed liturgies and rituals to serve not only as a reminder, but also somehow to connect spiritually with the power of the original gospel events. The current practice of the Church in the West reflects the penitential character of the Lenten season, with its use of the colour purple for vestments and the omission, except on festival days, of celebratory acclamations such as Allelluia and Gloria in Excelsis at the Eucharist. Along with the various liturgical emphases, the Church has encouraged Christians to observe Lent as an opportunity for an examination of their lives; urging penitence, almsgiving, and the seeking of a closer walk with God. A part of this has included the encouragement to abstain from something we hold to be pleasurable or important; and in the idea of giving something up for Lent we have the symbolic vestiges of the original, full-blooded Lenten fast. For many Christians of the early centuries, the development of liturgies and rituals was simply not enough. They felt that the institutional Church had become corrupt, and had lost its original vision. A substantial number of them took the wilderness experience literally and moved out into the desert, believing that only there could the essence of the gospel be recaptured in its purest form.

It was not obvious to me at the time, but looking back, I realize that I experienced something of this lack of connection between the symbolic action and its root for myself. I am probably not alone in having found Lent difficult to understand as a child. The many years I sang in the choir of my local church ensured that I had regular experience of the season, but it was very difficult to capture any sense of what it all really meant. The primary question seemed always to be: 'What are you going to give up for Lent this year?' The strong implication was that 'giving something up' was A Good Thing To Do, but I never really seemed to connect with the reason as to why this might be so. Somehow it was quite hard to see how my giving up chocolate (or even harder, potato crisps!) enabled me to share in the sufferings of Christ – whatever that meant. Easter promised chocolate eggs but it was a long, hard trek to get there – six weeks as compared to the four weeks of Advent. Lent lacked, for me, the anticipatory excitement of Advent, despite the fact that it culminated in Easter. The mood of the season was much more sombre, and it seemed to stretch before me like a wilderness which had to be crossed somehow before the gloom lifted and I could emerge into the light on the other side of Easter.

It was many years before I realized why there was such a difference in feel between the two seasons, even if the reason now seems obvious. Advent encapsulates the Israelite people's centuries of longing, watching and waiting through the long night of Old Testament history for the coming of the Messiah. It also anticipates our own watching and waiting as we look forward to the promised return of Christ at the end of time, even though we know neither the day nor the hour when he might come. But in both these dimensions, the long night of waiting moves inexorably towards the promise of new life and light encapsulated in history in the birth of Jesus at Bethlehem. Easter, too, celebrates glorious, miraculous new life and the birth of a new creation in the resurrection of Christ from death. But the only way we can get to that resurrection and truly to experience this new life is to walk faithfully the Lenten journey with Christ; and with Christ, we will find ourselves led inevitably through the wilderness to the cross.

Left to itself, human nature naturally shrinks from such a daunting prospect. We find it difficult to dwell on suffering, and will often put ourselves through extraordinary contortions in order to try and avoid it. And when we consider that the season of Lent – as does Advent – offers us a paradigm for the whole of life's journey, some of the many ways we adopt to avoid the challenges posed by the isolation of the wilderness become clear:

- We may overwork in order to avoid difficult relationships at home, or to try and reassure ourselves that we are useful and needed.
- We may sit for hours in front of a television screen, living our lives by proxy through the fictional characters we see there, rather than engaging directly with our own life issues.
- We may be terrified of boredom, and so fill our spare time with a constant round of frenzied and trivial activity.
- Through the internet, we may subscribe to the comforting illusion of never having to be alone; we can have access to information and 'company' twenty-four hours a day.

And perhaps, in our anxiety to deny the inner wilderness, we are only too ready to comply with such temptations, while our bodies and spirits succumb to the stress that those temptations inevitably bring. We may indeed become so accustomed to the sense of emptiness within us, that we fail to recognize it for what it really is. As the list above indicates, we may go to extreme measures to avoid this recognition, even at the cost of our physical, mental and spiritual health. But it is difficult for us to ignore such inner promptings indefinitely, even when things are running smoothly. In such times a niggling restlessness nudges at the

edges of our awareness, and a sense of the emptiness within makes us yearn for a deeper and lasting fulfilment. A
spiritual guide or companion may be of particular help
here; someone who knows us and is able to reflect our
struggles and avoidances back to us with an objective eye.

Although I was unaware of it at the time, this came very
close to the wilderness feel that Lent had for me as a child.
The wilderness is an inevitable part of the human experience of us all, and the invitation extended to us is to enter
into our own experiences of wilderness, resting patiently
and trustingly in it with Christ, and resisting the temptation
to avoid its challenges through self-diversion and needless
over-activity. For some this may involve embracing the
grief and mass of complex emotions and feelings that follow bereavement; for others it may involve living with the
pain and reality of physical or mental illness. Others may be
outwardly healthy, and yet experience a frustration and a
thwarting of their desires, which can lead, despite many of
the outward trappings of success, to disillusion and despair.
For these, the challenge is to acknowledge and own the
emptiness, resisting the temptation to cram it with false
securities and ego-boosting tricks. A number of the men I
met in my work in prison chaplaincy found themselves
thrust into the wilderness involuntarily. They were in a difficult environment, separated from their families; they had
time on their hands and not a lot to do all day. Many were
aware of guilt in their hearts, and found themselves asking deeper questions about life and belief than they had
ever done before. It was not unusual for people to come to
Christian faith in prison, and the time for reflection that a
grim prison environment made possible was sometimes the
springboard for a profound life change. Whatever our particular life circumstances, like Jesus, we will find that we
are driven out into the wilderness by the Spirit. We are

challenged to believe and trust that the wilderness has value and meaning in itself, and to rest patiently in the shadows, waiting for the strengthening and infilling of God.

❧

One of Hollywood's most enduringly successful films has been the 1946 classic, *It's a Wonderful Life*. The story follows the life of George Bailey, a young man growing up in the small town of Bedford Falls in the years before, during and just after the Second World War. Some years before the opening of the story, George's father had sacrificed most of his own money to found the Bailey Building and Loan Society, enabling the poor working people of the town to get out of the slums and to buy their own homes. This has made him a thorn in the side of Potter, a crooked business tycoon who owns the slums and everything else in the town and who is also on the board of the Building and Loan.

At the opening of the story, we are told that the young man George has become so disillusioned with his life that he is contemplating suicide. Before being sent to earth to try and save George, his guardian angel, Clarence, is shown a playback of George's life up to that point. What Clarence is shown first is a courageous and adventurous twelve-year-old, with huge plans to learn all he could at college and then travel the world. As the years progress, one by one George's dreams and plans are dashed. Through a chain of personal misfortunes, George and his wife Mary find they have to sacrifice almost everything they have in order to prevent the evil Potter completely taking over the town.

During the war, when George 'fights the battle of Bedford Falls', the pressure and dirty tricks from Potter are unrelenting. The final straw comes when, through the carelessness of George's uncle Billy, and unbeknown to George, a

huge sum of the Building and Loan's money falls into
Potter's hands. Potter holds on to the money, accuses
George of fraud, and calls in the police. At the end of his
tether, George flees, intending to take his life by jumping
into the river.

At the very moment George is about to jump, Clarence,
now in human form, jumps in first, and George dives in to
save him. Not surprisingly, George takes some convincing
that Clarence is his guardian angel! His mood has not
changed, and he tells Clarence that he wishes he had never
been born. Clarence takes him at his word, and George is
given a glimpse of the world as it would have been if he
had not been born. From the bleak picture he sees, he is
astonished to realize that there is a catalogue of positive
effects that his presence and actions have had on other
people at critical moments in their lives – effects of which he
had been totally unaware. George is finally convinced that,
despite the disappointment, the struggle and the frustration, his life has had real meaning and purpose. In tears of
gratitude and contrition, he prays to be able to live again.

Lent is supposed to be the time when we think of Jesus in
the wilderness. And the wilderness belongs to us. It is
always lurking somewhere as part of our experience, and
there are times when it is pretty near the whole of it. I'm
not thinking now of people being ostracized, or without
friends, or misunderstood, or banished in this way or that
from some community or other. Objectively . . . these
things happen to very few of us. Most people's wilderness is inside them, not outside. Thinking of it as outside
is generally a trick we play upon ourselves – a trick to hide
from us what we really are; not comfortingly wicked, but
incapable, for the moment, of establishing communion.
Our wilderness, then, is an inner isolation. It's an absence

of contact. It's a sense of being alone – boringly alone, or saddeningly alone, or terrifyingly alone.[2]

Hollywood ideas of theology and the afterlife may perhaps be questionable, but when compared with Harry Williams's account of the true meaning of Lent in *The True Wilderness*, this film hits very near the mark. As the story unfolds, we witness George's journey through his own personal wilderness. We experience with him the frustrations and disappointments, the thwarted ambitions and the restricted horizons his circumstances impose upon him. We feel with him the despair that strikes when his reputation seems to be irretrievably damaged, and all hope of love and happiness seems lost. Through the intervention of Clarence, George is enabled to draw back from suicide, confront his sense of inner isolation, and accept his life as the gift that in reality it is. George eventually triumphs through a return to his life as it is, not through an escape from it.

If our Lent has no awareness of this wilderness dimension, but focuses instead simply on the desirability of giving something up – or even its more positive counterpart, doing something especially constructive – we will miss the point and our deeper selves will remain untouched. Because, like George Bailey, we each carry our own wilderness around with us, we have no need to look beyond it to find the true meaning of Lent. Our primary task is to engage with our own experience of wilderness in whatever form it presents itself, wrestling with the problems it raises and resisting the temptation to take the easy way of escape.

꞊꞊꞊

And so we return to the defining event of the Lenten season. It is Jesus' time in the wilderness, rather than any symbolic actions adopted by us or by the Church corporately, which gives the season its meaning. Harry Williams again:

> This sense of being isolated and therefore unequipped, is a necessary part, or a necessary stage, of our experience as human beings. It therefore found a place in the life of the Son of Man. Because he is us, he too did time in the wilderness. And what happened to him there shows us what is happening to ourselves. Here, as always, we see in his life the meaning of our own.[3]

In the wilderness Jesus experienced loneliness and a terrible isolation. There were constant temptations to short-circuit the processes of self-emptying and trust-building; processes which provided the necessary preliminaries not only to his public ministry, but the blueprint for the whole pattern of his life.

The experience of Jesus here strikes a chilly chord in all of us, and he enters the wilderness as our representative. It is perhaps no wonder that we would prefer not to accompany him there but rather to skim quickly over the surface, not considering too deeply the feelings that may lurk beneath. A few years ago, a regular churchgoer celebrated the events of Holy Week in a church that was not her own. She was delighted and relieved when the minister decided to short-circuit the whole process and have the church celebrate Easter on Good Friday, ignoring the actual events of Good Friday altogether. Her comment was, 'It was such a relief – I wish the Church would do that every year!'

In the wilderness, Jesus was similarly tempted to take short cuts. Each time he withstood the temptation, claiming the Word of God as the foundation on which he stood. And Jesus here provides the pattern for our own experience, if we will let him:

And so, we are tempted of Satan. Tempted to give up, to despair. Tempted to cynicism. Tempted sometimes to cruelty. Tempted not to help others when we know we can, because, we think, what's the use. Tempted to banish from our life all that we really hold most dear, and that is love; tempted to lock ourselves up, so that when we pass by people feel, 'There goes a dead man.' And behind each and all of these temptations is the temptation to disbelieve in what we are; the temptation to distrust ourselves, to deny that it is the Spirit himself which beareth witness with our spirit. God in us.[4]

The symbol of the wilderness, then, running through the Lenten experience, becomes the crucible in which our hopes and desires, our motives and actions, are subjected to the intense fire of testing. If we are able to stand our ground, submitting to the process of purifying and cleansing and resisting the temptation to seek an easy escape, we may find that our vision is clarified and a new direction set. Writing somewhat prophetically himself, Winston Churchill said this of Moses and his personal time in the wilderness, before being called by God to lead the Israelites out of Egypt:

Every prophet has to come from civilisation, but every prophet has to go into the wilderness. He must have a strong impression of a complex society and all that it has to give, and then he must serve periods of isolation and meditation. This is the process by which psychic dynamite is made.[5]

For each one of us, as for Moses, for the Israelites and for Jesus himself, the wilderness may be a place where we find ourselves attacked at our points of greatest vulnerability.

But as God provided manna for the Israelites in the wilderness, and angels ministered to Jesus after his time of temptation, so we too have the promise of divine nurturing to sustain, strengthen and renew us.

❦

The wilderness is a powerful symbol not just for Lent, but for the whole of life. In its clear light our dross is stripped away and we are confronted with the truth – about God, and our lives in relation to him. In a paper entitled 'Wilderness – A Way of Truth', Laurens van der Post argues that the wilderness is a symbol through which all people have the possibility of recovering their lost capacity for religious experience:

> What wilderness does is present us with a blueprint, as it were, of what creation was about in the beginning, when all the plants and trees and animals were magnetic, fresh from the hands of whatever created them. This blueprint is still there, and those of us who see it find an incredible nostalgia rising in us, an impulse to return and discover it again. It is as if we are obeying that one great voice which resounds and resounds through the *Upanishads* of India: 'O man, remember.' Through wilderness we remember, and are brought home again.[6]

Ideas for Prayer and Reflection

Almighty God,
whose Son Jesus Christ fasted forty days in the
    wilderness,
and was tempted as we are, yet without sin:
give us grace to discipline ourselves in obedience to your
    Spirit

and, as you know our weakness,
so may we know your power to save;
through Jesus Christ your Son our Lord,
who is alive and reigns with you,
in the unity of the Holy Spirit,
one God, now and for ever.
Amen.

Collect for the First Sunday of Lent, *Common Worship*

❦

The desert is a 'land unsown', with no opening towards
the future. Israel had known it, the unforgettable desert
of their birth . . .

[In the desert, the Israelites] failed the test, and what was
in their hearts was sin: murmuring, lack of trust, despair,
turning in on themselves, rejection of the call to love,
betrayal of the covenant and refusal to see the desert as
the place for knowing the Lord and the way to the Land
of Promise. Yet this wilderness where they confronted
their sin and unfaith was also the place where they knew
the faithfulness of God. He led them, provided for them,
gave them bread from heaven and water from the rock,
and finally brought their children to the 'exceedingly
good land'. Israel 'looked steadfastly towards the wilderness' (Exod. 16:10) and there, in that unlikely place, they
saw the glory of God.

Maria Boulding[7]

❦

My heart was wilderness
I heard your voice;
my grief divided me
you held me close;
bitterness consumed me
you overflowed with trust;
I longed to be with you
you let me stay.

Janet Morley[8]

❦

Consider what circumstances and experiences at this particular stage in your life journey may constitute your own personal 'wilderness'. What are your feelings about this, and what is your attitude towards it? We are human, and tend to want to escape; but not all difficult circumstances are meant to be evaded. Bring your situation before God in prayer, and ask him to show you if this is a wilderness of *his* choosing.

❦

In prayer, ask God to bring back to your mind previous wilderness experiences. It is often easier to trace God's footprints in our lives in retrospect, so pray that God will remind you of his earlier working and leading in dark phases of your life. Give thanks for his constant and faithful presence, particularly at those times when that presence seems hidden from you.

❦

Merciful Lord
grant your people grace to withstand the temptations
of the world, the flesh and the devil,
and with pure hearts and minds to follow you, the only
   God;
through Jesus Christ our Lord,
Amen.

Post Communion prayer for the Third Sunday of Lent,
Common Worship

Scene 2

Darkness and Being Alone

One rainy, windswept Friday evening many years ago, I was battling through the London rush hour on my way to Ealing Abbey, where I and a number of other people were to stay for a silent weekend retreat. I was feeling very apprehensive, and did not know what to expect. I had never been on a retreat of any kind before, and in my previous experience of prayer and worship, silence had played only a minimal part.

Having misjudged the journey time, I arrived late. I had missed the first session, where people were welcomed to the Abbey and encouraged to introduce themselves to one another; dinner was nearly over and monks and visitors alike had already moved into silence. I was in a strange place, with people I did not know, and with apparently no means of getting to know anyone as we were not supposed to talk. With the silent weekend stretching ahead seemingly into infinity, at that moment I felt as lonely as I had ever done in my life.

The ripples and after-effects of that profound experience of prayer, silence and study of Scripture still resonate in my life today. When the retreat came to an end at lunchtime on Sunday and we were finally able to talk, I found that we had an ease and security in each other's company that belied the fact that we had only been together – in silence – for one short weekend. The conversations we were able to have I would only have thought possible within relationships of many years standing, and certainly could not have occurred had we simply spent the weekend trying to get to know each other through the more usual vehicle of speech. In fact, as most of our time had been spent either with our spiritual directors, in silent meditation in chapel, or in our own rooms, we had not spent the weekend trying to get to know each other at all. Against all expectations, the intense loneliness I experienced on arrival had been transformed into a profound solitude, the depths of which engaged me more deeply with my fellow human beings, rather than cutting me off from them.

This was my first experience of real silence and its most paradoxical quality; its ability to provide the ground for the development of deep knowledge and relationship. It was not only that this would not have been possible with words alone, but also the feeling that words would have actively hindered the process. And there was a further paradox; during the course of the weekend the intense loneliness I experienced on my arrival was transformed into a solitude which was alive with the riches of deep communion. This was a revelation to me, and was not something I could have foreseen in any way.

୧୫♣୨୭

One of the most remarkable things about this experience of solitude was that it occurred in the company of other people. Thomas Merton states that, while periods of physical solitude are vitally important,

> the truest solitude is not something outside you, not an absence of men or of sound around you; it is an abyss

opening up in the centre of your own soul. And this abyss
of interior solitude is a hunger that will never be satisfied
with any created thing.[1]

Merton continues that it is in this solitude, stripped of the
material supports we normally take for granted, that the
deepest growth and creativity can begin to find possibility
and form. He tends to use the terms 'loneliness' and 'solitude' interchangeably, but I feel they represent two very
different reactions to the experience of being alone. To be
lonely is to feel keenly the lack of normal human compan-
ionship and of those material comforts on which we have
come to rely, and to continue to yearn after that which we
have lost. An experience of solitude however, means we
have been able to relinquish our emotional hold on those
physical props on which we normally depend, and have
turned instead to the unsuspected riches and resources
which lie within us. The one experience creates restlessness,
anxiety and a pervading sense of loss; the other brings deep
peace, freedom from fear, and a sense of having connected
at a profound level with that which is most vital to life. But
these two experiences of being alone are not static states;
they form a spectrum along which we can move, as I discovered during my time at Ealing Abbey.

There are a myriad ways of being alone. My experience
was a voluntary one, but there will be many occasions in life
where our experience of aloneness will not be freely chosen,
and we may find ourselves frightened, kicking against its
constraints and demands. Serious illness, particularly if it
means having to spend time in hospital, can feel particularly
isolating. In the hospitals where I work as a chaplain, I meet
many people who are fearful and uncertain, disorientated
by the hospital routine and unsure and afraid about what is
going to happen to them. Apart from the anxieties raised by

their illness, the sudden loss of control of their life and the need to submit to the decisions of others can lead to feelings of real distress and alienation. And if all this happens to be combined with a bad prognosis, then the sense of loneliness and isolation can be overwhelming.

And yet this, too, has the potential to be turned towards the more positive end of the loneliness/solitude spectrum. Beverley Lancour Sinke, a cancer sufferer since 1983, describes how she tackled her feelings of panic and isolation during one particular phase of her treatment:

> I would search to find meaning in all of this – but it would take time and require patience. It was during this eye treatment that I further developed my 'inner universe.' I have a tendency to be claustrophobic so I would mentally remove myself . . . One of the places I chose to go was the golf course. I would practice my swing and play the golf holes over in my mind . . . Another place to which I would mentally escape was my sacred space. This God-space within, this inner universe, can take whatever shape we give it. My God-space took the form of a valley. This technique is simply an image-aid in helping us interact with a sometimes mysterious and unseen God. I need only be still and enter my valley to encounter my God who is for ever present there waiting for me. It is a comforting and healing place of retreat.[2]

We will encounter many other life experiences which face us with a sense of loneliness and isolation. For the many in our society today who are homeless, and for refugees cut off from the soil which nurtured them, this seems to be a profound and ongoing reality. And for all of us the experience of being misunderstood, and of attempting vainly to communicate our meaning and intentions to others, can sometimes create the feeling of being alone against the world.

These experiences are to some degree common to us all, and are part of the business of being human. The accounts of the experiences of people such as Beverly Sinke and the Beirut hostage Brian Keenan (of whom more later) show us the new life and hope which can be found in the most desperate and lonely of circumstances. And perhaps the real gift that the solitary religious offers to our world is to show, through a voluntary adoption of the solitary life, that all our experiences of loneliness and alienation are capable of transformation into something of infinite worth. For the rest of this chapter we will be looking at the lives of two such solitaries; St Cuthbert of Lindisfarne from the seventh century, and the twentieth-century Cistercian monk Thomas Merton, both of whom struggled in their different times and circumstances with the tension between the demands of the world, and their compelling desire for solitude.

৩৯৩

Cuthbert was born in 634 in Northumbria, probably into a noble family. In 651, while tending sheep by night, he had a vision in which he saw the soul of Aidan, monk of Iona and Bishop of Lindisfarne, carried up to heaven. Inspired by this vision, Cuthbert decided to become a monk himself, and he entered the Anglo-Irish monastery at Melrose under the spiritual guidance of the prior, Boisil. When Boisil died of the plague in 664 Cuthbert succeeded him as prior, and he continued Boisil's work of pastoral visiting and preaching in the surrounding district.

For many years there had been growing tension between those in the Church who followed the Celtic customs, and those who were more influenced by the Roman traditions from the continent. One of the chief differences between the two approaches lay in the fact that they celebrated Easter a week apart. This caused great difficulties at the Northumbrian court where King Oswiu followed the Celtic ways and his queen, Eanflaed, conformed to the teachings of Rome. A unified date for Easter needed to be found, and a resolution came with the Synod of Whitby in 664 when the decision was made to follow Roman practices. Although Cuthbert had been brought up in the Celtic ways he accepted the decision of the Synod, and when moving to Lindisfarne as prior sometime in the 670s, he reformed the monastic rule in accordance with the Roman tradition.

From within his many responsibilities and intensely active pastoral ministry, Cuthbert felt an increasing pull towards the solitary life of a hermit. He moved first to the little island just off Lindisfarne now known as St Cuthbert's Isle, and later to the much more remote island of Inner Farne, just off the coast to the south of Lindisfarne:

After many years in the monastery he finally entered with great joy and with the goodwill of the abbot and the monks into the remoter solitude he had so long sought, thirsted after, and prayed for. He was delighted that after a long and spotless active life he should be thought worthy to ascend to the stillness of divine contemplation . . . To learn the first steps of the hermit's life he retired to a more secluded place in the outer precincts of the monastery. Not till he had first gained victory over our invisible enemy by solitary prayer and fasting did he take it upon himself to seek out a remote battlefield farther away from his fellow men . . . The Farne lies a few miles to the south-east of Lindisfarne . . . Cuthbert was the first man brave enough to live there alone.[3]

His solitude was to be rudely shattered, however. In 685, at the insistence of the Northumbrian king Ecgfrith, Cuthbert was reluctantly persuaded to leave his island and take on the role of bishop:

> Shortly afterwards there was a great synod presided over by Archbishop Theodore of happy memory, in the presence of King Ecgfrith, at which Cuthbert, by general consent, was elected Bishop of Lindisfarne. Letters and messengers were sent to him repeatedly, but he refused to move. The King himself and that most holy bishop, Trumwine, with numerous devout and influential personages sailed across, knelt down and adjured him by the Lord, and wept and pleaded with him, until at last he came forth very tearful, from his beloved hiding place and was taken to the synod. Very reluctantly he was overcome by their unanimous decision and was compelled to submit to the yoke of episcopacy.[4]

As a bishop, Cuthbert seems to have been most effective, and was reputed to possess the gifts of prophecy and healing. He also managed to find the difficult balance between the preservation of his ascetic way of life, while at the same time pursuing an active pastoral ministry of teaching, preaching and visiting.

But his time as a bishop was to be short. Early in 687, in failing health, Cuthbert finally laid down the burdens of high office. Sensing that death was approaching, he withdrew once again to the island of Inner Farne, where he died on 20 March at the age of fifty-three.

❦

Thomas Merton was born in Prades, France, in January 1915, and suffered a difficult and unhappy childhood. His mother Ruth died of cancer when he was six years old, and for much of the next nine years he lived an itinerant and unsettled life as he moved from place to place with his father, who was an artist. Merton showed considerable early promise in both languages and the visual arts, and was deeply influenced by his father's work. In his adult life, this artistic gift would be expressed first through painting, and later, photography. The death of his father – also from cancer – when Merton was fifteen, left the boy insecure and confused, searching for some meaning and direction in his life.

After pursuing a hedonistic path in his late teens and early twenties, Merton experienced a dramatic religious conversion while he was a student at Columbia University. He was received into the Roman Catholic Church at the age of twenty-six, and three years later he entered the Cistercian Abbey of Gethsemani in Kentucky, to continue his spiritual search as a Trappist monk and later, priest.

The change was dramatic. From the extroversion and gregariousness of his previous life, Merton entered a world of harsh austerity, committed to solitude and silence. But the medieval structure of the Abbey's life may well have spelt security for one who had no stable home in his childhood, and who was orphaned young. Gethsemani, despite the testing and challenging nature of its way of life, was a place of healing for Merton. There were periods of painful struggle during the 1950s, but during the last decade of his life Merton found both a new compassion for himself and others, and a deepening concern with the wider issues of the world. Along with writings on prayer and spiritual life, he wrote prolifically on subjects such as the arms race, racial concerns and world poverty.

Apart from his calling as monk and priest, Merton was, above all, a writer. It is therefore supremely ironical that he entered an order vowed to silence – whether of the spoken or the written word. For some time indeed, Merton assumed that his career as a writer was at an end; then a few volumes of his poetry were successfully published, and his autobiography, *The Seven-Storey Mountain*, became a bestseller. Through his continued writing in solitude, the Trappist monk was reaching people in a way he may never have achieved had he remained outside the monastery.

As the years progressed, Merton's needs changed. His need for the security the Cistercian structure provided gradually diminished, and his longing for greater solitude on the one hand, and wider contacts with the outside world on the other, correspondingly increased. During his last few years, Merton was given permission to live as a hermit in a hut in the Abbey grounds. This was not total isolation; he was still part of the Abbey's life, and was dependent on it for food and drink. He engaged in correspondence, and was able to receive visitors. All this was necessary to Merton, but the real periods of solitude that the hermitage gave him were also vital for his further spiritual and religious growth. Under this more relaxed regime, Merton was free to go to conferences and meetings outside the Abbey, and it was at a conference in Bangkok in 1968 that he died, tragically and accidentally, of electrocution. Like Cuthbert before him he was fifty-three years old.

❦

Although separated in time by thirteen centuries, there are a number of striking resonances between the lives of St Cuthbert and Thomas Merton:

- Both responded as young men to the call to serve God as a monk.

- Both found that their ministry began to extend beyond the monastery walls, and they found themselves engaging in their different ways with a wide public.
- As time went on, both were increasingly drawn towards the solitary life; a desire which arose from within the context of their active ministry, and was felt to be, to a considerable extent, in tension with it.
- For both men this tension was never entirely absent. Merton wrongly assumed that on entering Gethsemane his life as a writer would be over. But the tension between his longing for solitude, and his need to reach out to others through his writings or in person, remained a constant throughout the rest of his life. As we saw with Cuthbert, his attempt to live the solitary life on the island of Inner Farne was dramatically interrupted when he was physically compelled to return to the mainland and serve the Church as a bishop. Two years of effective but relentless activity fatally undermined his health, and he finally returned to Inner Farne for the last two months of his life.

The pattern that emerges here in the lives of these two men seems to suggest that the states of solitude and activity are both vital, and are inextricably linked. Solitude that exists purely for its own sake and has no contact with the world will prove sterile; while self-generating activity that has no time or space for solitude will eventually, and damagingly, burn itself out. In the experiences of Cuthbert and Thomas Merton, it would appear that within the apparent darkness and emptiness of true solitude lies the potential of a deeper and richer interaction with the world than would have been possible if they had spent their lives in ceaseless activity. In the same way, if their seeking after solitude had simply signified a selfish wish for a quiet life, then their powerful gifts of ministry would have found no channel of effective expression. As with them, so also with us. Our times of solitude and silence feed our periods of creative activity, which in its turn drives our roots ever deeper into that deep well in the centre of our own soul where we encounter the living God. Merton captures the dynamic of the ebb and flow of this interrelationship, and stresses what must be its chief aim and purpose:

> We do not go into the desert to escape people but to learn how to find them; we do not leave them in order to have nothing more to do with them, but to find out the way to do them the most good. But this is only a secondary end. The one end that includes all others is the love of God.[5]

Ideas for Prayer and Reflection

O Christ,
who suffered the pain of misunderstanding,
rejection and unjust death;
lighten the darkness of our loneliness,
and transform it into the solitude
which knows the radiance of your resurrected Presence.
For your name's sake we pray.
Amen.

Barbara Mosse

Even the most beautiful community can never heal the wound of loneliness that we carry. It is only when we discover that this loneliness can become sacrament that we touch wisdom, for this sacrament is purification and presence of God.

If we stop fleeing from our own solitude, and if we accept our wound, we will discover that this is the way to meet Jesus Christ. It is when we stop fleeing into work and activity, noise and illusion, when we remain conscious of our wound, that we will meet God.

He is the Paraclete, the One who responds to our cry, which comes from the darkness of our loneliness.

Jean Vanier[6]

•❈•

Ask God for the courage not to flee from those moments when fear, or boredom, or a sense of your own aloneness make themselves felt in your heart. Resist the temptation to crowd such moments of awareness out with distractions and diversions. Pray that God will stand alongside you in your loneliness, and help you to experience it as an opportunity of realizing his deeper presence.

•❈•

Even though I walk through the valley of the shadow of death I will fear no evil; for you are with me, your rod and staff – they comfort me.

Psalm 23.4

And after (Jesus) had dismissed the crowds, he went up the mountain by himself to pray. When evening came, he was there alone.

Matthew 14.23

•❈•

My Lord God, I have no idea where I am going. I do not see the road ahead of me. I cannot know for certain where it will end . . . Nor do I really know myself, and the fact that I think I am following your will does not mean that I am actually doing so. But I believe that the desire to please you does in fact please you, and I hope that I have that desire in all that I am doing . . . I know that if I do this, you will lead me by the right road though I may know nothing about it. Therefore will I trust you always though I may seem lost in the shadow of death. I will not fear, for you are ever with me, and you will never leave me to face my perils alone.

Thomas Merton

Scene 3

Darkness and Unknowing

> So set yourself to rest in this darkness as long as you can, always crying out after him whom you love.
>
> *The Cloud of Unknowing* (late fourteenth century)

Some time ago, my husband and I had the disturbing experience of temporarily losing our dog on a country walk. Everything had begun as usual, with Frodo gambolling and frolicking a short distance ahead of us on the path through the woods, stopping and checking every minute or so to make sure we were still in sight. Some time later while we were deep in conversation, we realized that Frodo had not only vanished, but that there was no sound of his movement in the woods. We started the usual ploys of calling and whistling, and when they proved fruitless, we split up to search in different directions. With a mounting sense of anxiety I retraced our steps, and it was with considerable relief that I met a couple who asked if I had lost a dog. 'He's sitting by the side of the path about two hundred yards back,' they said. 'We thought his owners were probably ahead, so we tried to persuade him to come on with us. He was friendly, but quite determined to stay where he was.' Sure enough, there was Frodo sitting by the path, and there was a relieved reunion on both sides. The relevance of this episode will, I hope, become clear as we continue our explorations.

❧❧❧

The short quotation from *The Cloud of Unknowing* with which this chapter began indicates a form of prayer which has been present in the Church's experience from earliest times, but which the Church has often regarded with ambivalence and uncertainty. Popular religion and spirituality has generally taken the way of overt prayer, praise and supplication, expressing itself through the medium of the senses. Valuable and important as this way has been, it has tended to develop at the expense of the more negative way – the *via negativa* as it came to be known. This is a darker, more hidden way, and it recognizes that any words we may use to describe God, or any experience of him we may discern through our human senses, cannot begin to capture the wonder and reality that is God in his fullness. Because God is utterly beyond the range of our human senses, we cannot really know him through feeling, thinking and seeing. It follows that waiting upon God in this way is likely to feel like waiting in darkness, with little or no sensible awareness of his presence.

But this darkness, I would suggest, is precisely the place where God is to be found, and it is shot through with the radiance of his uncreated light. This light is invisible to our senses, and was dubbed paradoxically a 'dazzling darkness' by the poet Henry Vaughan. We have already explored some examples in earlier chapters, and it is good to remind ourselves of the place of this creative and awe-inspiring darkness in the biblical accounts. In Genesis, the pre-creation darkness is suggestive of the womb which brings forth teeming, abundant life through the action of God's impregnating Word. Moses, as we saw, approached Mount

Sinai and 'the thick darkness where God was' (Exod. 20.21), and found it to be the place of both revelation and communion. Paul in his epistle to the Romans indicates that the Spirit will lead our prayer to a depth which is beyond our human words and comprehension:

> Likewise the Spirit helps us in our weakness; for we do not know how to pray as we ought, but that very Spirit intercedes with sighs too deep for words. And God, who searches the heart, knows what is the mind of the Spirit, because the Spirit intercedes for the saints according to the will of God.
>
> *Romans 8.26–7*

In the New Testament, a withdrawal into silence and solitude is seen as the necessary foundation to any major initiative in ministry or proclamation. John the Baptist serves his long apprenticeship in the desert before embarking on his public ministry of preaching and baptizing. Jesus is driven by the Spirit into the wilderness for forty days before beginning his ministry, and during that ministry he regularly withdrew from other people for solitary nights of prayer. Saul had a three-day period of silence and solitude imposed upon him after his conversion on the road to Damascus. During this time he neither ate nor drank and was physically blind; symbolic perhaps of the radical stripping away of all that he thought he knew, and the depth of his consequent transformation. In the first chapter of his epistle to the Galatians, Paul states that on receiving his commission from Christ, he did not immediately go up to Jerusalem to present himself to the other apostles, but 'went away at once into Arabia' for an unspecified period of time (Gal. 1.17).

The Church Fathers and Mothers were disciples of the early Christian centuries who left the towns and cities in increasing numbers. They sought a life of prayer which was more authentic than they felt was possible since Christianity had become the official state religion, and had acquired many of its trappings. They sought out a life which taxed them, physically, mentally and spiritually; they renounced the normal securities and comforts of daily life in order to place their trust and reliance in God alone. To worldly eyes they achieved little, if anything; but to the eyes of faith they conveyed the context and concept of eternity. Helen Waddell, writing in the introduction to her translation of the writings of the Desert Fathers, points out that these men and women taught humanity how to live in the context of eternity. By turning their backs on the 'light' of their day and deliberately embracing the dark and the unknown, they paradoxically enriched the life they denied in ways which still speak profoundly to us today.[1]

One of these Fathers, the fourth-century Gregory of Nyssa, admitted that the dark way is not for the newcomer to Christianity:

Scripture teaches . . . that religious knowledge comes at first to those who receive it as light. Therefore what is perceived to be contrary to religion is darkness, and the escape from darkness comes about when one participates in light.[2]

But as the life of faith grows and deepens, the visible light diminishes as the disciple begins to discern more clearly the God who is beyond human experience:

For leaving behind everything that is observed, not only what sense comprehends but also what the intelligence thinks it sees, it keeps on penetrating deeper until . . . it gains access to the invisible and the incomprehensible, and there it sees God. This is the true knowledge of what is sought; this is the seeing that consists in not seeing, because that which is sought transcends all knowledge, being separated on all sides by incomprehensibility as by a kind of darkness.[3]

In an important recent book,[4] Melvyn Matthews argues that the Church has lost sight of this darker, mystical way of prayer. Understanding 'mysticism' to imply an inner contemplative consciousness, Matthews states that an urgent recovery of this contemplative awareness is necessary for the very survival of the Church:

The moment at which the mystical way will open up as a possibility for the Christian believer has always been a moment of grace, but it has become increasingly necessary for the life and health of the Church, particularly the western Church, to allow that moment to emerge and to seek to create the conditions under which it will emerge.[5]

In a Church which, like the world, is all too often lured by the attractions of materialism, the teaching of the Desert Fathers may startle and shock. It does so because as western men and women of the twenty-first century, we have long been used to living on the surface of things and have become increasingly divorced from our inner depths. For Matthews, the chief symptom of this dislocation between surface and depth lies in an amassing of 'things' – possessions and insurances of various kinds which we treat as if ours by right. We have lost the concept of stewardship, but most of all, we have lost the awareness of our natural frailty and vulnerability before God. We tend to live our lives as if trying to obliterate that reality from our consciousness, bolstering ourselves with false securities.

Those who insisted on living their lives in close awareness of this abiding but uncomfortable reality stand out like dark and glistening threads woven down through the generations. If we follow one such thread we see how Gregory of Nyssa and the other Desert Fathers spark our awareness. The torch is passed on through the austerities of the lives of Celtic saints such as Columba and Aidan in the seventh and eighth centuries, Bernard of Clairvaux in the twelfth, to Julian of Norwich and the anonymous author of *The Cloud of Unknowing* in the fourteenth century. The thread continues through Meister Eckhart in the fourteenth and fifteenth centuries, St John of the Cross in the sixteenth, and on into the twentieth century with the contemplatives Henri Nouwen and Thomas Merton:

> The curious state of alienation and confusion of modern man in modern society is perhaps more bearable because it is lived in common, with a multitude of distractions and escapes – and also with opportunities for fruitful action and genuine self-forgetfulness. But underlying all life is the ground of doubt and self-questioning which sooner or later must bring us face to face with the ultimate meaning of life.[6]

The writings and experiences of these people across the centuries have the power to provoke and disturb us to the extent that we are already aware, consciously or unconsciously, that the way we live is not the way things are meant to be. We dimly suspect that we are superficial creatures, and that we are attempting to satisfy ourselves with the ephemeral which can only lead ultimately to disillusion and death. But we are afraid of the depths, fearing them to be dark and destructive; so we skate along on the surface, dislocated from the riches and resources in the depths of our inner being.

Matthews states that we need to get to a point where we realize another way of living is not only possible, but necessary for our survival.[7] The Desert Fathers, and later the Celtic saints, moved away from the society of their time in order to discover their true selves before God. In their experience society, and the Church, had become so worldly that such discovery had become impossible; to remain would have meant alienation, a total cutting-off from the true reality that lay in the depths.

To respond to the call to the inward depths runs counter to the modern mentality which seeks satisfaction and enjoyment from what is immediately on offer. This 'normality' we tend to take for granted and without thought; but people who have experienced a sudden and unexpected change in their life situation have found themselves confronted with a very different reality. This may happen through the unexpected onset of critical illness, or a sudden bereavement. People who have experienced being taken hostage have found themselves catapulted into a situation where the relationships and trappings of modern life have been suddenly and violently stripped away. Through the shock of being captured at gunpoint, the unimaginable horror of solitary confinement, torture and the real threat of death at any moment, many have been compelled to take the journey inward and have discovered to their surprise that a new and unsuspected depth of reality began to emerge. The Beirut hostage Brian Keenan, speaking of himself and his fellow hostage John McCarthy, compares their experience with that of their captors:

Our world was not the monotone morality which defined

and limited theirs. Even in these most deprived conditions we found within ourselves and within those shared
discussions a more valuable and richer world than we
had conceived of before. We were beginning to learn our
freedom . . . Captivity had re-created freedom for us. Not
a freedom outside us to be hungered after, but another
kind of freedom which we found to our surprise and
relish within ourselves.[8]

⁅✲⁆

If we reflect on extreme experiences such as these, we
perhaps get some clue as to why the Church so desperately
needs to recover this contemplative awareness within its
own life and witness. When a bow is drawn across a string
of a violin, all the other strings will vibrate sympathetically,
providing a range of harmonics that fill out and enrich the
original note. In a similar way, the hidden treasures of
this dark tradition have the ability to draw sympathetic
resonances from within the depths of our own souls, and if
we are able to acknowledge and attend to these resonances,
our lives will be immeasurably the richer. While comparatively few will find themselves faced with the hostage
experience, many more will face sudden illness; few will
escape the experience of bereavement, and death is the one
certainty in life for everyone.

For all of us, the complex tapestry of everyday living
with its periodic experiences of waiting and helplessness,
boredom, abandonment and unbelief, is an inescapable
reality. So much of modern life exacerbates these feelings.
The child moves from the close family atmosphere of the
primary school and feels loneliness and a lack of belonging
in the vast anonymity of the new comprehensive; the young
man feels increasingly cut off from his family as his firm

demands longer and longer working hours; the middle-aged find themselves suddenly made redundant with their skills and experience no longer welcome in the market place; those living in isolated rural areas despair when their local bank is closed in the name of greater efficiency and supposed improvements in customer service. And while the benefits of computer technology may be considerable, the illusion of intimacy created through websites and chat rooms can be a dangerous one, masking the reality of our deepening isolation from one another as we sit in our solitary rooms, transfixed to our screens.

The resurrection of Christ is the keystone of our faith, but if we focus exclusively on the triumphant, relentlessly homing in on the resurrection while ignoring the cross, we will inevitably convey a God who is two-dimensional and unconnected with the real experiences of peoples' lives. What is more, we too will experience a faith that has nothing to say to us of any real depth. Such a faith may leave us defenceless when we encounter our personal moments of crisis, and leave us struggling to help those going through their own times of darkness. A close friend recently lost her husband after a prolonged and painful illness. After his death, comments by some well-meaning fellow Christians to the effect that now she would be able to get her life back together again were acutely distressing, as were the actions of those who avoided her because they did not know what to say. We need to realize that there are times when words, however well-meaning, may not only be unhelpful but actually harmful, and that there are no magic solutions for our deep pain. It is far from easy to sit alongside someone in their pain with nothing to offer in the way of words, but offering them instead an acceptance of their distress in all its unresolved rawness. But there are times when words need to give way to silence, and the mystery of God which that silence encompasses; because it is in that silence, beyond all our thoughts, words and actions, that the healing and transforming power of God carries out its hidden and miraculous work.

❦

The present-day Carmelite nun Ruth Burrows writes in her spiritual autobiography *Before the Living God*,[9] that the way that God has chosen to lead her in life has been almost entirely by a sense of his absence. The intensity of this negative experience is perhaps unusual, and she attributes her experience to a variety of emotional, psychological and spiritual factors springing from her genetic make-up and upbringing. The path for Ruth Burrows has been intensely painful but this is no unacknowledged atheism; the sense of God's absence has been powerfully charged and deeply meaningful – even if at times only in hindsight – and she remains deeply grateful for the path along which she has been led. If we are able to embrace such experiences when they occur in our own lives, we have a natural point of empathy with those many in our world who seek for God, but struggle to find him.

The author of *The Cloud of Unknowing* understands well the human experience of emptiness, the temptation we have to panic and the attempts we make to fill the apparent vacuum with comforting activity. Here the author addresses our problem in the context of prayer:

Leave aside this everywhere and this everything, in exchange for this nowhere and this nothing. Never mind at all if your senses have no understanding of this nothing; it is for this reason that I love it so much the better. It is so worthy a thing in itself that they can have no understanding of it. This nothing can be better felt than seen; it is most obscure and dark to those who have been looking at it only for a very short while. Yet to speak more truly, a soul is more blinded in experiencing it because of the abundance of spiritual light than for any darkness or lack of bodily light.[10]

In words and phrases that are mysterious, paradoxical and strange to twenty-first-century ears, the author of *The Cloud* points us to the reality of God which inspires our words, thoughts and actions, but is ultimately beyond the furthest limits of anything our human imagination and intellect can construct. While using to the fullest possible extent the gifts and abilities we have been given, our eternal happiness lies in our realization and acceptance of their limitations. Our fulfilment will come not only through responding to the light which we can see, but also by waiting patiently in faith and trust in the purely spiritual light of God, which seems as darkness to us because it lies beyond the reach of our human senses.

And so we wait in faith and trust; and in that experience I am brought back graphically to the incident of our lost dog with which I began this chapter. When Frodo realized that we had become separated, and that he could no longer sense our presence near him, his reaction was to stay where he was and wait quietly. He is a young and very enthusiastic dog, and might have been expected to rush round frantically trying to find us. But he seemed to know instinctively that the quickest and surest way to be found was to stay precisely where he was without struggle or panic, resisting any temptation to try solutions of his own – he would not go with the couple who encouraged him to follow them. Obviously I am not imputing human levels of understanding and awareness to our dog, but there does seem to be a sense in which what Frodo seemed to know instinctively, we have to learn repeatedly through painful experience. In our times of darkness and unknowing, in personal prayer and in the wider prayer that is Life, we are encouraged to wait patiently and without resistance for the coming of our God, and to trust that this particular experience of darkness is his chosen crucible for our healing and transformation.

Ideas for Prayer and Reflection

Mysterious God,
Whose silence speaks louder than our words,
and whose darkness guides more surely than our light;
May we trust you in cloud and in sunlight,
in the interplay of Word and Silence,
Until we know as we are fully known.
Through Jesus Christ our Lord.
Amen.

Barbara Mosse

There are two sorts of darknesses; some unhappy, and others happy: the first are such as arise from sin, and these are unhappy, because they lead . . . to eternal death. The second are those which the Lord suffers to be in the soul, to establish and settle her in virtue; and these are happy, because they illumine the soul, fortify her, and give her greater light.

Miguel de Molinos, *A Spiritual Guide Which Disentangles the Soul*,
Book 1, chapter VI

When you encounter a 'dry' phase in your prayer life, be open to the possibility that this dryness may be a means of God leading you into a deeper experience of his love. Try to resist the temptation to revert to familiar 'props', which may crowd out the still, small voice you are seeking. When the child is learning to cycle, stabilizers may be necessary; but there comes a time when the stabilizers must go in order for the child to ride freely. So discard your stabilizers, relax, and let the darkness of God surround and support you.

Lift your heart up to God with a humble impulse of love; and have himself as your aim, not any of his goods . . . When you first begin . . . all that you find is a darkness, a sort of cloud of unknowing; you cannot tell what it is, except that you experience in your will a simple reaching out to God. This darkness and cloud is always between you and your God, no matter what you do, and it prevents you from seeing him clearly by the light of understanding in your reason . . . So set yourself to rest in this darkness as long as you can, always crying out after him whom you love. For if you are to experience him or to see him at all, insofar as it is possible here, it must always be in this cloud and in this darkness.

The Cloud of Unknowing, Chapter 3

When in your prayer you find yourself in unfamiliar territory, you may find it helpful to experiment with some nonverbal form of expression, such as painting, or moulding with clay. Some abstract works of art can be a useful vehicle

for meditation during these times of dark prayer, and may
encourage you to stay with God in the darkness into which
he has led you.

O God my dark my silence
whose love enfolded me
before I breathed alone
whose hands caressed me
while I was still unformed
to whom I have been given
before my heart remembers
who knew me speechless
whose touch unmakes me
whose stillness finds me
for ever unprepared

                Janet Morley[11]

Scene 4

Darkness and Disability

But we have this treasure in clay jars, so that it may be made clear that this extraordinary power belongs to God and does not come from us. We are afflicted in every way, but not crushed; perplexed, but not driven to despair; persecuted, but not forsaken; struck down, but not destroyed; always carrying in the body the death of Jesus, so that the life of Jesus may also be made visible in our bodies . . . So we do not lose heart. Even though our outer nature is wasting away, our inner nature is being renewed day by day. For this slight momentary affliction is preparing us for an eternal weight of glory beyond all measure.

2 Corinthians 4.7–10, 16–17

Throughout history, humanity has strived after the illusion of physical immortality. Our television screens today are full of advertisements offering ways to beat the process of ageing; a face-lift here, a small nip-and-tuck there, and hey presto! You too can enhance your attractiveness and 'freeze' your age at twenty-five, even though you may be well into middle age! For those of more limited means, there are a myriad of face creams and other beauty products on offer. And even though in this litigious age they may only promise to banish the *appearance* of ageing, the illusion is still the same; if you work hard enough at it, you really *can* live for ever. We live in an age which seeks to convince us that we can defy the reality of death, and encourages us to conduct our lives as if physical immortality was ours for the choosing. But however much we may buy into the illusion, the only certainty that can be said of each one of us is that one day, we will die.

With this preoccupation with the quest for physical perfection and a halting of the ageing process, it is perhaps not surprising that society's attitude to disability is deeply ambivalent. Society easily assumes that those with physical, mental and emotional disability must necessarily be lacking in their ability to live life to the full, and that consequently their 'quality of life' – whatever we may judge that to mean – must be severely compromised. Alongside the many wonderful benefits that have come to us through recent developments in medical science, there are undoubtedly others which cause grave concern because of the assumptions which appear to lie behind them. The routine screenings offered to expectant mothers today are able to reveal a variety of potential health problems in the unborn child. If a so-called defect is found, such as Down's Syndrome or spina bifida, it is not unusual for the mother to be encouraged to have an abortion on the grounds that the child would be unlikely to have any real quality of life. One woman I know refused – despite considerable pressure – to have any screenings at all during her pregnancy. Her reason for this was that she was determined to keep the child whatever problems might be found, and that there was therefore no point in having the screenings, which in themselves carried a small risk to her unborn child.

As well as raising huge questions as to the criteria which are used to determine and assess a person's quality of life, such an attitude itself leads to further questions. If an unborn baby found to have a condition such as Down's Syndrome is not considered worthy of life, what does this also say of our society's attitudes to those who, for one reason or another, become disabled later in life?

❦

As a new Christian, I remember being very powerfully moved by the real-life story of a young woman called Joni (pronounced Johnny) Eareckson. Back in 1967, Joni was a typical seventeen-year-old American teenager, growing up as the much-loved youngest daughter of a deeply Christian family. She was attractive and artistically gifted, outgoing and popular, and she loved riding and everything to do with horses. The upbringing she shared with her sisters was adventurous. Joni's father taught his children geography and geology during 'survival' backpack outings in the desert or the mountains, and these excursions helped to instil in Joni a deep love for God and his creation.

One glorious July evening, with the setting sun turning the water a glowing, fiery red, Joni dived into the murky waters of Chesapeake Bay:

> In a jumble of actions and feelings, many things happened simultaneously. I felt my head strike something hard and unyielding. At the same time, clumsily and crazily, my body sprawled out of control. I heard or felt a loud electric buzzing, an unexplainable inner sensation. It was something like an electrical shock, combined with a vibration – like a heavy metal spring being suddenly and sharply uncoiled, its 'sprong' perhaps muffled by the water. Yet it wasn't really a sound or even a feeling – just a sensation. I felt no pain.[1]

In the space of a mere sixty seconds, Joni had experienced a diving accident which left her totally paralysed from the shoulders down. In that instant her young life was transformed from one of vigorous activity and independence, to a state of utter helplessness in which she was unable to do even the smallest thing for herself. Her early days and weeks were a bleak fight for survival; surgery was needed and she struggled to hold on to life.

Once the initial crisis was over and the doctors grew more confident that Joni was not going to die from her injuries, then other feelings and emotions started to come into play. Joni found herself swinging between the heights of hope and elation, and the depths of despair. Would she ever be able to walk again? Why had God allowed this dreadful thing to happen to her? Promises in Scripture that everything works for good for those who love God, promises which she had never previously questioned, now seemed nothing but a cruel mockery. In the early months Joni found it impossible to reconcile herself to her condition. She prayed that she might die, and when this did not seem to be happening, she asked a close friend to give her an overdose of pills to put her out of her misery. The friend stood by Joni, continuing to visit her through the months of anguish, suffering terribly herself through the emotional blackmail Joni used in her repeated pleas to her to help her to end her life.

The confusion continued. As one expression of her anger against God and her rejection of his promises, Joni had immersed herself in the thought and writings of some of the great atheistic thinkers including Sartre, Hesse and Marx. But she was surprised to find that these brought her no enlightenment; they seemed only to add to the confusion. Paradoxically, Joni found that her act of rebellion, far from leading her to solutions away from God, actually led her back to him. She began to sense for the first time since her accident that God was not only real, but that he had never left her and was actively at work in her life and present situation. She found herself reminded of a prayer she made shortly before her accident, forgotten until that point: *Lord, do something in my life to change me and turn me around.* Joni realised, shockingly, that the accident and what followed may have been God's response to that prayer. Through her quadriplegia, she was being given the chance to rediscover the love of God anew, and to experience life with him without any of the distractions and trappings which we normally take for granted and which so often block our relationship with him.

It was not to be a totally unbroken upward pathway from then, but Joni did find that, although still confused, her confusion now leaned more towards trust than to doubt. Slowly, she began to feel that God did indeed have a plan for her life, and that, mysteriously, the accident had become part of that plan. As time went on she rediscovered her artistic gift, drawing this time with a pencil held in her mouth rather than her hands. She began to be asked to speak of her experiences and her vision of God within them, first to small groups, then to larger gatherings and eventually on national television. The gifted and somewhat headstrong teenager who prayed – without knowing what she meant – that God would turn her life around, had become an evangelist of humanity and conviction, willingly sharing her story with others to the glory of God.

One of the most challenging things about Joni's message is her belief that it was not enough for her simply to get to a point of putting up with what had happened. She needed to come to a place of genuine, heartfelt thankfulness that what had happened was being used by God as an important part of his plan and that her injury was not a tragedy, but a gift. This runs counter to humanity's natural perceptions, both inside and outside the Church. Her experience speaks to us with conviction because her position has been grappled for painfully, through intense struggle and suffering. There is no glib denial; she has faced the aw(e)ful reality head-on and emerged the other side with a clarified vision:

> It's a dangerous misunderstanding of the Bible to say categorically that it's God's will that everyone be well. It's obvious that everyone is not well . . . We're trying for perfection, but we haven't attained it yet. We still sin. We still catch colds. We still break legs and necks . . . The more I think about it, the more I'm convinced that God doesn't want everyone well. He uses our problems for his glory and our good . . . If I'd still been on my feet, its hard to say how things might have gone. I probably would have drifted through life – marriage, maybe even divorce – dissatisfied and disillusioned . . . I wouldn't change my life for anything . . . I even feel privileged . . . I'm really thankful (God) did something to get my attention and change me.[2]

Whether or not the echo is a conscious one, Joni's thoughts here are resonant of those of C. S. Lewis as he describes them in *The Problem of Pain*, and which we encountered first in the chapter on 'Darkness: The Place of Revelation'. Lewis observes that the human spirit, without any experience of pain or discomfort to challenge it, will not even begin to try to surrender self-will, as it sees no reason to do so:

> God whispers to us in our pleasures, speaks in our conscience, but shouts in our pains: it is His megaphone to rouse a deaf world.[3]

The idea that personal suffering can exist, not necessarily as an affront to the divine purpose but as a vehicle of it, is certainly in evidence in the biblical narrative. Earlier in this book we considered the situation of the man blind from birth found in John 9, where Jesus tells the scribes and the Pharisees that the man's blindness was not because of his or his parents' sin, but so that the greater glory of God may be shown. In the opening quotation at the beginning of this chapter, Paul makes reference to the fact that he and his fellow-Christians are 'always carrying in the body the death of Jesus, so that the life of Jesus may also be made visible' in their bodies. Here, the suffering is seen, not as an affront to God, but rather as a mysterious and powerful means by which the love of God is disseminated in the world. Further on in 2 Corinthians, Paul takes this concept one stage further:

> Therefore, to keep me from being too elated, a thorn was given me in the flesh, a messenger of Satan to torment me . . . Three times I appealed to the Lord about this, that it would leave me, but he said to me, 'My grace is sufficient for you, for power is made perfect in weakness.'
>
> *2 Corinthians 12.7b–9*

Paul has been describing to the Corinthians his experiences of fourteen years previously, when he 'was caught up into Paradise and heard things that are not to be told, that no mortal is permitted to repeat' (2 Cor. 12.4). It is in the context of these visions that Paul goes on to speak of the Lord's allowing him to be inflicted with 'a thorn in the flesh', in order to prevent him from becoming too carried away on account of the revelations. There have been many theories as to what form this thorn in the flesh took, but this discussion is irrelevant to our perspective here. The point is that, whatever Paul's particular thorn in the flesh was, he experienced it as something which on three occasions God refused to take away, because he deemed it necessary for Paul's own good. And even more than this; it was precisely in this weakness that God's power was to be most clearly manifest.

⟨❧⟩

Duncan was a highly intelligent young man who had won a place at a top university to read for a four-year honours degree. Three years and one term into the course, and with the winning-tape in sight, Duncan was struck down with manic depression. The year that followed was the blackest he had ever known, as his moods swung like a pendulum between elation on the one hand and suicidal depression on the other. His Christian faith during this time was no help to him; none of the tried and tested methods of prayer or Bible study seemed able to connect with the heights or depths of his experience. Believing that God had abandoned him, Duncan attempted to take his own life.

Thanks to the skill and understanding of a good psychiatrist, Duncan's life was saved and a vital corner was turned. Having lost his faith completely, he slowly and painfully began to discover that the God whom he had come to believe did not exist was not only intensely real, but was by his side in the darkness. Having found himself in a position where the idea of belief was a cruel mockery, Duncan's faith began to come to life again. Exactly a year after his initial collapse he was able to return to the university and finish his course, emerging with a first-class honours degree.

Thirty years on, manic depression remains a reality in Duncan's life, and ups and downs continue to be a normal part of his life experience. His condition is well controlled through medication and intermittent therapy, and things have never since descended to the level of hopelessness and despair which characterized that first year of illness. In all of this, Duncan acknowledges the importance of the help of doctors, the support of family and friends, and an understanding church fellowship.

But Duncan has been able to move way beyond mere tolerance of an extremely distressing condition; in some mysterious way it has become a positive asset. In writing papers on his own experience of manic depression, he has been able to offer help and support to other sufferers and those who love and care for them. He has responded to invitations from church groups to talk about his experiences. In recent years he has come to feel that his illness, far from being an imposition, has become an integral part of who he feels himself to be, as a Christian and as a human being. To seek to 'get rid' of the manic depression, were such a thing possible, would be like cutting off a part of himself.

Do not worry about tomorrow, for tomorrow will bring worries of its own. Today's trouble is enough for today.

Matthew 6.34

Duncan found over a prolonged period of time that the best way of living as a manic depressive was to give heed to Jesus' teaching in the Sermon on the Mount. This meant living with openness and transparency, attending faithfully to the tasks of the day and leaving the rest aside:

MD offers us the chance to develop a self-discipline which we might never have found elsewhere. If we know that it can strike at any time without notice, we learn to keep our affairs up to date and in order so that damage is minimal when it does. For instance, we pay our bills, we answer our letters, we do the housework and odd jobs. Some find it helpful to keep a 'do' list of outstanding tasks, crossing them off with great satisfaction as each is completed.

Not having a secret to hide reduces tension. Hiding MD means putting up a front of normality, being misunderstood until we collapse with no one any the wiser or in a position to help.

Facing up to MD within ourselves means we can start to live easily with ourselves. As we seek to build up our inner resources we embark on a voyage of self-discovery . . . and we end up all the richer.[4]

ᏻ✤ᏺ

The experience of deafness must be one of the most difficult of all afflictions for a musician. Unlike the percussionist Evelyn Glennie whom we considered earlier, the composer Ludwig van Beethoven never became reconciled to his condition. The problem began to manifest itself in 1798, when the composer was twenty-eight years old, and by 1820 his deafness was almost total. But as early as 1802, the condition was bad enough for Beethoven to write a letter to his brothers, intended to be read after his death, in which he describes his despair on realizing that his deafness could not be cured:

> I must live almost alone like one who has been banished. I can mix with society only as much as true necessity demands. If I approach near to people a hot terror seizes

upon me and I fear being exposed to the danger that my condition may be noticed. Thus it has been during the last six months which I have spent in the country . . . what a humiliation for me when someone standing next to me heard a flute in the distance and I heard nothing, or someone heard a shepherd singing and again I heard nothing. Such incidents drove me almost to despair, a little more of that and I would have ended my life – it was only my art that held me back.[5]

Although this is not a conscious cry to God, it is hard not to be struck with resonances here to some of the feelings expressed in Psalm 22:

But I am a worm, and not human;
scorned by others, and despised by the people.

Psalm 22.6

This feels quite close to Beethoven's

I must live almost alone like one who has been banished . . . If I approach near to people a hot terror seizes upon me.[6]

There are no indications in what we know of Beethoven's life and experience to suggest that he was ever consciously aware of any potential hidden 'treasure' in his deafness. On the contrary, the condition caused him to despair so deeply that it drove him to consider suicide. And yet, during the very same six months in the country referred to in his letter, Beethoven wrote his Second Symphony, a piece full of exuberant joy and vibrant life. In this music, the light and life which bursts forth totally transcends the grip of the darkness which was threatening to overwhelm and destroy its composer. At the point at which he wrote the letter to his brothers, Beethoven claims that the one thing that held him back from suicide was the realisation that he had more music to write, and that it was impossible to leave the world until he had brought forth all that he felt was within him. Despite the bleakness of the inner struggle and the desperation of his feelings, the forces of life and creativity emerged triumphant.

꩜

[Jacob] got up and took his two wives, his two maids, his eleven children, and crossed the ford of the Jabbok. He took them and sent them across the stream, and likewise everything that he had. Jacob was left alone; and a man wrestled with him until daybreak. When the man saw that he did not prevail against Jacob, he struck him on the hip socket; and Jacob's hip was put out of joint as he wrestled with him. Then he said, 'Let me go, for the day is breaking.' But Jacob said, 'I will not let you go unless you bless me.' So he said to him, 'What is your name?' And he said, 'Jacob.' Then the man said, 'You shall no longer be called Jacob, but Israel, for you have striven with God and with humans, and have prevailed. Then Jacob asked him, 'Please tell me your name.' But he said, 'Why is it that you ask my name?' And there he blessed him. So Jacob called the place Peniel, saying, 'For I have seen God face to face, and yet my life is preserved.' The sun rose upon him as he passed Penuel, limping because of his hip.

Genesis 32.22–31

This strange and enigmatic tale has puzzled and fascinated biblical scholars for centuries. Jacob is seeking to move on from a past in which he has cheated his twin brother Esau out of both his birthright and their father's blessing. Just prior to this incident, in an attempt to appease his brother, Jacob has sent on ahead several droves of animals as propitiatory gifts. Finally, he sent his wives, children and servants across the ford of Jabbok in preparation for the next stage of the journey to the Promised Land. When Jacob was left alone, a man appeared and wrestled with him in the darkness until daybreak. It is clear from the biblical account that both parties accept that Jacob's mysterious protagonist is God, and that the struggle that marks their encounter is one in which physical injury, a new name, and God's blessing are inextricably linked.

The meaning of this tale is so elusive that it is open to a huge variety of interpretations. Perhaps one such is that Jacob, far from being hindered by the injury inflicted, is somehow strengthened and enabled through it to move on in his journey. Along with the disability came the granting of a new name – Israel – indicating for the biblical writer the double striving that has taken place between God and Jacob in this encounter. And finally, with the dawning of the day comes God's blessing, and Jacob limps onwards towards the rising sun.

꧁❈꧂

Perhaps, after all, the term 'disability' is simply a question of degree. We may not suffer from any discernible injury, yet in our seeking after God we are all handicapped to some extent. Each of us will have situations and factors in our lives which disturb and confront us, which overturn our carefully laid plans and challenge us with the possibility of whole new ways of living and being. With many of the smaller challenges we encounter day by day we may feel it is possible to evade or ignore them, sidestepping them as we attempt to continue travelling down our pre-planned path. But sometimes the challenge is too great for that, and experiences such as paralysis, mental illness, blindness or deafness compel an encounter which cannot be ignored. The sharp and double-edged nature of such Jacob-like encounters with God is expressed graphically by the university lecturer John Hull, totally blind at the age of forty-eight after many years of deteriorating eyesight. In this extract from a letter, he responds to an enthusiastic fellow Christian who has offered him the supposed guarantee of a miracle healing:

> I do not interpret my blindness as an affliction, but as a strange, dark and mysterious gift from God. Indeed, in many ways it is a gift I would rather not have been given and one that I would not wish my friends or children to have. Nevertheless, it is a kind of gift . . . I have learnt that since I have passed beyond light and darkness, the image of God rests upon my blindness . . . I am a Christian like yourself. My Christian life has been deepened since I lost my sight. This loss has helped me to think through many of my values in living, and in a way I have learnt a greater degree of intimacy with God.[7]

Wherever our experience places us along the spectrum of human suffering, C. S. Lewis's picture of the megaphone of human pain challenges us to accept and respond to the dark and mysterious gifts we are given. If we are able to rise to the challenge, we have the promise that we will discover the darkness to be a mine of unsuspected resources. We are indeed clay jars, and we contain within ourselves a hidden treasure offering unimaginable opportunities for growth and transformation through the mysterious workings of the indwelling God of love:

> We speak God's wisdom, secret and hidden, which God decreed before the ages for our glory . . . As it is written,
>
>> 'What no eye has seen, nor ear heard, nor the human heart conceived, what God has prepared for those who love him' –
>
> these things God has revealed to us through the Spirit; for the Spirit searches everything, even the depths of God.

1 Corinthians 2.7, 9–10

Ideas for Prayer and Reflection

Good Friday

Christ our victim,
whose beauty was disfigured
and whose body torn upon the cross;
open wide your arms
to embrace our tortured world,
that we may not turn away our eyes,
but abandon ourselves to your mercy,
Amen.

Janet Morley[8]

Jesus reached out and touched the leper, the crippled, the social outcast, when others, even his closest disciples, turned away. Ask God in prayer to gently reveal to you an aspect of disability that makes you fearful and causes you to turn away, and ask him to help you to look at the fear with his eyes. Consider recording your thoughts and feelings in a journal, or through painting or drawing. Try to relax and be as free as you can – your picture is for your own personal expression and prayer, and does not have to be an artistic masterpiece! You may find it helpful to share some of your reflections with your spiritual director or soul friend.

༺✿༻

Jesus said, 'I came into this world for judgement so that those who do not see may see, and those who do see may become blind.'

John 9.39

༺✿༻

In its intimacy, its openness, its weakness and its vulnerability, blindness can offer a sort of archetype of the future. Blindness offers this in many ways, not only in itself but also through awakening the tactile and acoustic worlds. It can be a way . . . of understanding and overcoming the great historic divisions of humanity into the weak and the strong, those in wealth and those in poverty, those in sickness and those in health. To grasp this is to turn the stigma of blindness into a calling, from stigma to stigmata. The same is true of any experience of human weakness, which is why the kingdom of God is to be found amongst children and amongst the poor.

John Hull[9]

༺✿༻

We shrink from the disabled for so many reasons. A cold shiver unsettles our inner complacency; if it can happen to them, what is there to say it couldn't happen to us? We are tempted to turn our backs, hugging our comfort-blankets of illusion around us. If we deny our kinship and common humanity with the disabled, then perhaps we shall be safe . . .

. . . and there is more. If we acknowledge our kinship and reach out in love and acceptance, we open ourselves to the painful reality of our own woundedness, to the pain, disability and weakness which is a part of the fallen nature we carry with us every day of our lives. Whether we happen to be disabled or able-bodied, disability is a form of sacrament, a visible reminder of this universal truth: that no one is completely whole, and that we each, like Jacob, limp towards the sunrise with God's mysterious blessing upon us.

'Lord, when was it that we saw you hungry and gave you food, or thirsty and gave you something to drink? And when was it that we saw you a stranger and welcomed you, or naked and gave you clothing? And when was it that we saw you sick or in prison and visited you?' And the king will answer . . . 'Truly I tell you, just as you did it to one of the least of these who are members of my family, you did it to me.'

Matthew 25.37b–40

Scene 5

Darkness and Suffering

Simon was a highly talented musician. He had done his training some years ago at one of the big music colleges, and had graduated with the highest honours in a number of different musical disciplines. But there was an underlying loneliness and unhappiness in him; a single man who longed to be married, he struggled also to find his niche in the musical world. In many ways, his brilliance worked against him; there were so many fields in which he was professionally gifted, he found it difficult to settle fully in any one of them. I came to know him when he was organist and musical director at our local church, and the rest of his time was split between piano teaching and freelance orchestral work.

Time passed, and our work took us in different directions. I heard with interest that Simon was greatly enjoying furthering his musical studies, going to university and completing an MA, with a PhD and a period of study abroad in prospect. Pastoral work with students at the university was also giving his life a purpose and focus that previously it had seemed to lack, and he sounded much happier within himself. It was with a real sense of shock therefore, that I heard some time later that Simon had been diagnosed with terminal cancer, and had been given two years to live. He was thirty-four years old.

What happened during the next two years proved to be

an inspiration for all who knew Simon, and an induction into some of the profound and mysterious workings of God. He had always been a deeply committed Christian, but now the way he lived his Christian life became imbued with an urgency and sense of purpose he had never experienced before. With his family, his friends and the students in his care, Simon was totally open about both his illness and his faith; urging us all not only to live for the satisfactions of the present moment, but to see our lives in the fuller context of the God who created us and calls us back to himself. He experienced difficult times as his health deteriorated, and as the debilitating treatments left him progressively weaker. But he communicated his message with love, pastoral concern and humour, and with an honesty and fearlessness that posed a profound challenge to the fears of the rest of us. There was no denial in Simon's attitude to his approaching death; rather, he was able, in Christ, to look the reality full in the face, and find in it a focus and meaning for his life. We spoke on the telephone a few weeks before he died, and he reassured me that he was at peace with himself and with God, and was ready to go and be with him. He also said that, if he were given the choice of having the last two years of his life over again, exactly as they had been, or living in good physical health to the ripe old age of ninety, he would choose to have the last two years again. Simon was no masochist. It was just that through his illness in those final two years things at last began to fall into place, and he found a meaning, purpose and fulfilment he had been searching for all his life. The uncertain, unhappy and somewhat lonely man that Simon was when I first met him had been transformed into an evangelist of deep conviction, able to communicate the power and truth of the gospel in sincerity and love.

The question of the origin and meaning of suffering is as old as humanity, and it is tackled in many and various ways throughout the biblical narrative.[1] Alongside the prophet and the priest, ancient Israel acknowledged the place of another role – that of the wise:

> . . . for instruction shall not perish from the priest, nor counsel from the wise, nor the word from the prophet.
>
> *Jeremiah 18.18*

It was recognized that God had created the world out of chaos and imposed divine order, and the task of the wise was to instil or point to that divine order amidst the chaos of everyday activity, in both individuals and in society as a whole. Wisdom was a natural and necessary complement to the Law, in that both sought to achieve and maintain the divine order which had been imposed in the creation.

Consequently, the early wisdom literature does not question the moral order of the world, or the belief that human beings are rewarded with what they deserve. The equation is a simple one; the righteous will prosper, and the wicked will be punished:

> The Lord watches over the way of the righteous, but the way of the wicked will perish.
>
> *Psalm 1.6*

> The good obtain favour from the Lord, but those who devise evil he condemns. No one finds security by wickedness, but the root of the righteous will never be moved.
>
> *Proverbs 12.2–3*

By the time of Ecclesiastes, however, the ground was decidedly shifting. The neat certainties of earlier times were being turned on their heads, and giving way to something altogether darker and more pessimistic:

> I saw all the deeds that are done under the sun; and see, all is vanity and chasing after wind.

Ecclesiastes 1.14

> There is a vanity that takes place on earth, that there are righteous people who are treated according to the conduct of the wicked, and there are wicked people who are treated according to the conduct of the righteous.

Ecclesiastes 8.14

Between these two extremes of the equation of just deserts on the one hand, and the chaos resulting from a total absence of moral order on the other, lies the book of Job.

The Prologue and Epilogue (Job 1–2; 42.7ff.) of the book come originally from an older tale, and demonstrate clearly the belief we have been considering; that the righteous will be rewarded and the good punished. Job is a righteous man, and consequently he enjoys the fruits of God's blessing in the abundance of his family and material possessions. In the setting of the divine court, Satan (an adversary, rather than the devil of later theology), asks some difficult questions regarding the relationship of human beings to God, using Job as an example. Just suppose, says Satan, that Job were to lose all that he had – wealth, children, status and physical health – would he still remain upright and blameless?

Does Job fear God for nothing? Have you not put a fence

around him and his house and all that he has, on every side? You have blessed the work of his hands, and his possessions have increased in the land. But stretch out your hand now, and touch all that he has, and he will curse you to your face.

Job 1.9b–11

God agrees to the testing of Job, and in a dramatic reversal of fortune Job loses his property and children, his physical health and his high status in the community. His wife speaks for the old beliefs; in her view this devastating loss must reflect the loss of God's blessing, so the only thing left to do is to curse God and die (Job 2.9). But Job refuses to despair, saying that it makes no sense to trust God only when things are going well. He remains faithful to God and preserves his integrity.

The Dialogue which follows however (Job 3–27; 29–31), is believed to come from a later period and presents a far more complex picture. At the outset Job curses, not God, but the day of his birth:

Let the day perish on which I was born, and the night that said, 'A man-child is conceived.' Let that day be darkness! May God above not seek it, or light shine on it. Let gloom and deep darkness claim it. Let clouds settle upon it; let the blackness of the day terrify it.

Job 3.4–5

The scene which follows is depicted as a court case, with Job as the plaintiff challenging the traditional Jewish orthodoxy represented by the views of his three friends. Each side adopts a pre-determined position and attempts to silence the opposition by the force of their own arguments. The

whole case revolves around the entirely new concept of the
existence of innocent suffering in the world, and the nature
of God in relation to that suffering. Job may not deny God,
but he questions passionately:

> Why do the wicked live on, reach old age, and grow
> mighty in power? Their children are established in their
> presence, and their offspring before their eyes. Their
> houses are safe from fear, and no rod of God is upon
> them.
>
> *Job 21.7–9*

> Why are times not kept by the Almighty, and why do
> those who know him never see his days? . . . From the city
> the dying groan, and the throat of the wounded cries for
> help; yet God pays no attention to their prayer.
>
> *Job 24.1, 12*

Job feels utterly alone; his wife and his friends do not
understand him, and God remains silent. It is in the experience of God's silence that Job is forced to make the crucial
decision; will he deny the God who seems to have deserted
him, or will he continue to trust, even though he gets no
satisfactory answers? It is in this defining moment that Job
enters fully into the darkness of the God who is mystery.
His triumphant assertion, 'In spite of . . . I believe', from the
depths of his sense of rejection brings him once more into
an awareness of God's presence.

But even here, there are no clear-cut and easy answers.
Instead of responding directly, God overwhelms Job,
relentlessly piling up question upon question of his own:

> Where were you when I laid the foundation of the earth?
> Tell me, if you have understanding . . . Have you com-

manded the morning since your days began, and caused
the dawn to know its place? . . . Have the gates of death
been revealed to you, or have you seen the gates of deep
darkness? . . . Do you know the ordinances of the heavens? Can you establish their rule on the earth? . . . Is it by
your wisdom that the hawk soars, and spreads its wings
towards the south? Is it at your command that the eagle
mounts up and makes its nest on high?

from Job chapters 38 and 39

God's response to Job – and the message of the book as a
whole – gives no answer to the question of innocent suffering. What Job receives instead is a breathtaking declaration
of the sheer majesty, glory and creative power of God.
There is an agnosticism about the book of Job; the author,
wrestling with the question of unjust suffering, does not
have a ready answer. But what he does say is that, in spite
of suffering, it is still possible for human beings to know
God and to be in relationship with him. This conclusion
became absorbed into Jewish religious consciousness, and
was carried through into the Christian experience:

> For I am convinced that neither death, nor life, nor
> angels, nor rulers, nor things present, nor things to come,
> nor powers, nor height, nor depth, nor anything else in
> all creation will be able to separate us from the love of
> God in Christ Jesus our Lord.

Romans 8.38–9

We have considered Job at some length because the
book's message is timeless. In our troubled and at times
capricious world today we face precisely the same concerns; the question as to why we suffer, and the constant
challenge to seek God in spite of the suffering, and to trust

that in him we can discover the peace, order and stability that otherwise eludes us.

❦

The fourteenth-century mystic and theologian Julian of Norwich lived in dark and troubled times. War with France, three epidemics of the Black Death and the poverty and starvation that gave rise to the Peasants' Revolt formed the backdrop to her life and work, together with the beginnings of the Great Schism in the Catholic Church which led to the setting up of two rival popes in Avignon and Rome.

On 8 May 1373, Julian received an extraordinary series of divine revelations on the Passion and death of Christ – or 'showings', as she called them – while she was apparently dying of a serious illness. After her recovery she spent many years as an anchoress, living a solitary life in a small cell attached to St Julian's church, pondering the meaning of her 'showings' and offering spiritual counsel to those who sought her help. These seekers must have brought the troubles of the age right to her door, yet despite the turmoil of the world outside her cell her message was one of abounding confidence, with Christ's promise that 'all shall be well, and all shall be well, and all manner of thing shall be well'.[2]

But Julian seems not to have been alone in detecting the hidden light of Christ within the darkness of her time. The contemporary writer Sheila Upjohn has spent many years researching and speaking about the life of Julian. So struck was she with the contrast between Julian's message of deep optimism and the darkness of her age that she decided to explore something of the creative life in Norwich during Julian's lifetime:

In Julian's day, the square mile of the walled city of Norwich held another twenty-one religious houses, as well as the cathedral, together with no less than sixty-three parish churches. During her lifetime nearly all of them were being enlarged and refurbished. Norwich people were at work painting frescoes, and rood screens, and altar pieces. They were carving in wood and in stone – bosses and tracery and saints and fonts and angel-roofs and misericords. They were embroidering sumptuous vestments and altar frontals. They were designing and making stained glass: the Norwich workshops were famous. Norwich goldsmiths and silversmiths were making chalices and patens. Scribes were illuminating manuscripts. They were building churches in daring and original styles. The place was alive with people making beautiful things.[3]

The astonishing thing about this discovery, was that all this was achieved against such a bleak background by a small number of illiterate, poorly fed and badly housed craftsmen who had a life expectancy of not much more than fifty. Julian's day has often been compared to our own in its violent and unsettled nature. This may be superficially true, but the creative response of the people then seems strikingly different from that which we see now. The praise-giving and life-affirming beauty and craftsmanship of the fourteenth century, giving glory to God in spite of the tragedies and uncertainties of life, has largely gone. In its place has come a sense of hopelessness and of nature some-how turning in on itself, reflected perhaps in the piles of bricks, pickled animals and unmade beds that are part of the produce of today's artistic world.

Sheila Upjohn concludes that, while some similarity may exist between the external world of the fourteenth century and that of today, the interior world of the people must have been very different. Much of our artwork today reflects back to us a loss of faith, and a sense of revulsion against the human condition. In Julian's day, the faith of the people seemed to give them a grasp of their true nature under God, and an ability to make some kind of sense of the horrors that surrounded them. They were able to find treasure in the darkness, and this was reflected abundantly in the creative beauty they produced.

❦

While this may be something of a prevailing trend, it would nevertheless be a mistake if we failed to acknowledge the many lights which do glimmer in the darkness. Today, there are countless examples of such treasure-seeking happening spontaneously in a myriad different ways.

Richard is a married man in his fifties who has suffered from manic depression for many years. While wrestling with the constraints of his condition, he has produced written material in which he willingly puts the fruit of his struggles at the service of other manic depression sufferers, and those who care for them.

The world-famous cellist and conductor Mstslav Rostropovitch was stripped of his citizenship and exiled from his native Russia for daring to stand up and challenge Stalinist oppression. When asked how he felt about the suffering that he and so many of his friends had endured, his response was that he was not angry; he believed that the creation of music of real depth and beauty was only possible when it had been forged in the crucible of suffering. He speaks here of his fellow countryman, the composer Shostakovitch:

> If [Shostakovitch] had not been so badly treated, especially in 1949 and 1950 when his music was banned and

he had no royalties, no commissions, no money for food, I am sure he would have lived longer and composed more. But would the music have been of such depth? I think not. I think about my American friends: Aaron Copeland, Lenny Bernstein. Phenomenal talents! Geniuses, even! But in their music, no suffering. Shostakovitch turned our country's history into symphonies.[4]

When the terrorists struck on the morning of 11 September 2001, the then Archbishop of Wales, Rowan Williams, was attending a meeting of Church leaders a few blocks away from the World Trade Center. While we consider one or two aspects of his meditation here, his moving and challenging reflection on that disaster cries out to be read, pondered and prayed over in its entirety.[5]

At the beginning of his meditation, Williams highlights a chilling paradox by focusing on two different forms of 'last words': those messages sent by passengers on the planes to their loved ones in the last desperate minutes, and the religious words of exhortation used to fortify the terrorists as they faced a so-called martyr's death, taking so many others with them. Williams comments that, while the language of religion is used as an encouragement to mass murder, the non-religious language used in the passengers' final messages 'are testimony to what religious language is supposed to be about – the triumph of pointless, gratuitous love, the affirming of faithfulness even when there is nothing to be done or salvaged'.[6]

In darkness as deep as this the treasure will not be easy to find, and may not be where we would most expect to find it. Williams concludes the preface to his meditation:

After the 11th, what are we supposed to learn? That's the

question to which I keep returning, and which fuels this meditation. Whatever the outcome of the military action, whatever your views on the rights and wrongs of the reaction of the USA and its allies, that question remains for us. I'm conscious of using 'we' and 'us' a lot in these thoughts, meaning the whole of our Anglo-American world of which I'm not a detached observer gifted with superior morality any more, I suspect, than you are, reader. This 'we' needs, God knows, time and opportunity to grieve; but time and opportunity also to ask whether anything can grow through this terrible moment. I hope the answer is yes.[7]

The experience of good somehow being forged out of the dark crucible of suffering is one which recurs throughout history, and yet it is an experience we should approach with great care and a sense of awe. It is all too easy to speak glibly of evil giving way to good, and darkness to light, without having any concept or feeling of what the lived experience of deep suffering actually means. Such a superficial approach may lead us to the conclusion that in certain circumstances, God actually causes people to suffer in order that their lives may be somehow bettered by the experience. The problem here lies not only in what this says about our concept of God; it is that many people's experience of suffering leaves them feeling battered, not bettered. For every person enabled to rise to the challenge posed by suffering, there are others who have found themselves crushed by it. The question of suffering and its potential for the creation of light in and through the darkness remains a challenge and a paradox.

❧

There are no easy answers. The suffering of Christ has been the inspiration through the centuries for those martyrs who willingly gave their lives for the faith, and whose blood was proclaimed as 'the seed of the Church'. Christ's suffering has also provided the pattern for those called to the mysterious path of vicarious suffering, whereby one individual is some-how enabled to bear the weight of suffering rightly belong-ing to another. In all our pain, the suffering of Christ is surely the key to whatever solution there is. The answer may well lie beyond our present horizon, but it is to the cross itself that we must cling as the source of our life and hope.

Ideas for Prayer and Reflection

Almighty God,
whose most dear Son went not up to joy but first he
    suffered pain,
and entered not into glory before he was crucified:
mercifully grant that we, walking in the way of the cross,
may find it none other than the way of life and peace;
through Jesus Christ your Son our Lord,
who is alive and reigns with you,
in the unity of the Holy Spirit,
one God, now and forever.
Amen.

Collect for the Third Sunday of Lent, *Common Worship*

Take a few moments to find a position where you can be comfortable, yet alert. Relax any tension in your muscles and begin consciously to deepen your breathing. In prayer, allow God, if he will, gently to reveal to you an area of unresolved hurt and suffering. Try not to fight against it but simply imagine his presence with you in the darkness, knowing and trusting that with him, the dawn will come.

❦

Man has places in his heart which do not yet exist, and into them he enters suffering in order that they might have existence.

Leon Bloy[8]

❦

On the man blind from birth (John 9):

What should strike us is Jesus' initial refusal to make the blind man's condition a *proof* of anything – divine justice or injustice, human sin or innocence. We who call ourselves Christian have every reason to say no to any system at all that uses suffering to prove things: to prove the sufferer's guilt as a sinner being punished, or – perhaps more frequently in our world – to prove the sufferer's innocence as a martyr whose heroism must never be forgotten or betrayed. If this man's condition is to have a symbolic value – and in some sense it clearly does in the text – it is as the place where a communication from *God* occurs – the opening up of something that is not part of the competing systems operated by human beings.

Rowan Williams[9]

❦

His broken body hangs on the wood
limp
dirty
covered with blood
ugly with wounds;
his face lined with agony,
no beauty,
no comeliness:
a man of sorrows.

And during all the time he hung there the woman
was beside him.

Mary was there,
standing at the foot of the cross,
a sign of hope, of trust, of love.
She stood firm,
this silent woman of compassion,
not crushed,
not fleeing from the pain.

Jean Vanier[10]

Can we think about our focal symbol, the cross of Jesus, and try to rescue it from its frequent fate as the banner of our own wounded righteousness? If Jesus is indeed what God communicates to us, God's language for us, his cross is always both ours and not ours; not a magnified sign of our own suffering, but the mark of God's work in and through the deepest vulnerability; not a martyr's triumphant achievement, but something that is there for all human sufferers because it belongs to no human cause.

Rowan Williams[11]

Lord, you did not come to explain away my suffering or remove it. You came to fill it with your presence. Be present to me, may my heart so overflow with your love that I am able to love you in return. Amen.

Brendan O'Malley[12]

Scene 6

Darkness: Passion and Death

Then the soldiers led him into the courtyard of the palace . . . and they called together the whole cohort. And they clothed him in a purple cloak; and after twisting some thorns into a crown, they put it on him. 'Hail, King of the Jews!' They struck his head with a reed, spat upon him, and knelt down in homage to him. After mocking him, they stripped him of the purple cloak and put his own clothes on him. Then they led him out to crucify him . . . It was nine o'clock in the morning when they crucified him. The inscription of the charge against him read, 'The King of the Jews'.

Mark 15.16–20, 25–6.

Many churches today offer people a pattern of services in Holy Week which make it possible to travel with Christ through the events of his passion, culminating in the crucifixion on Good Friday. To enter with commitment into the drama of Holy Week can be both a powerfully moving and yet ambivalent experience. While we are aware that the events of Christ's passion and death lie at the very heart of our faith, we tend to view the events leading up to the resurrection with some uneasiness. On the one hand we are human, and our instinct is to shy away from such intense suffering, preferring to direct our gaze quickly beyond it to the perceived safety of the resurrection where all is well again. In an earlier chapter I referred to the woman who was so relieved when her church decided to short-circuit the process and celebrate the resurrection on Good Friday. Although this may have offered short-term relief, the discomfort experienced by staying with Christ during the Holy Week journey is more than offset by the indescribable richness and depth to be found there. In the years when I have been unable for one reason or another to take part in the complete Holy Week sequence, I have felt deprived and strangely lacking, as if I had missed out on something of vital importance.

We are not alone in our ambivalence; those closest to Jesus in his life on earth also had difficulty in staying with him when the going got difficult:

Then Judas Iscariot, who was one of the twelve, went to the chief priests in order to betray him to them.

Mark 14.10

Peter said to him, 'Even though all become deserters, I will not.' Jesus said to him, 'Truly I tell you, this day, this very night, before the cock crows twice, you will deny me three times.'

Mark 14.29–30

All of them deserted him and fled.

Mark 14.50

[Peter] began to curse, and he swore an oath, 'I do not know this man you are talking about.' At that moment the cock crowed for the second time.

Mark 14.71–2

While Matthew and Mark describe a number of women looking on from a distance when Christ is crucified, John's Gospel places several of the key women and the beloved disciple very close to the foot of the cross:

> Meanwhile, standing near the cross of Jesus were his mother, and his mother's sister, Mary the wife of Clopas, and Mary Magdalene. When Jesus saw his mother and the disciple whom he loved standing beside her, he said to his mother, 'Woman, here is your son.' Then he said to the disciple, 'Here is your mother.'

John 19.25b–27a

As Christians we believe that Christ suffered and died for us. But there have been people, scattered throughout Christian history, who have been able to move beyond mere mental acceptance and to enter directly into the experience of Christ's sufferings. Most of us have shrunk from the idea of such raw exposure to Christ's pain. For the remainder of this chapter we are going to consider one thread which can be traced through the centuries; giving us a glimpse of the impact of the passion on some of those who did not shrink away, and to ask whether such experiences contain unsuspected treasure that could assist us in our own journeys.

The Dream of the Rood[1] is an Anglo-Saxon poem that was discovered in the tenth century, but may have been written a century earlier. After urgently commanding the attention of his hearers, the dreamer continues:

> It seemed to me that I saw a wondrous tree spreading

aloft spun about with light, a most magnificent timber. The portent was all covered with gold; beautiful gems appeared at the corners of the earth and there were also five upon the crossbeam.

Very quickly, the dreamer realizes that this jewel-encrusted tree is indeed the cross on which Christ died:

However, through the gold I could discern the earlier aggression of wretched men, in that it had once bled on the right side. I was altogether oppressed with anxieties; I was fearful in the presence of that beautiful sight . . . at times it was soaked with wetness, drenched by the coursing of blood, at times adorned with treasure.

What is striking about this poem is the stark conjunction of light and darkness, beauty and fear, blood and gold. More startling still is the next stanza, when the tree itself begins to speak, telling how it was cut down and fashioned by 'strong enemies' into an instrument of torture and execution. The cross then takes up the familiar story, describing the crucifixion as an act totally under the command of Christ:

Then I saw the Lord of mankind hasten with much fortitude, for he meant to climb upon me. I did not dare then, against the word of the Lord, to give way there or to break when I saw the earth's surfaces quake . . . The young man, who was almighty God, stripped himself, strong and unflinching. He climbed upon the despised gallows, courageous under the scrutiny of many, since he willed to redeem mankind. I quaked then, when the man embraced me; nonetheless I did not dare to collapse to the ground . . . I had to stand fast.

The poem continues with a consideration of the image of
Christ and the cross suffering together:

They pierced me with dark nails: the wounds are visible
upon me, gaping malicious gashes . . . They humiliated us
both together. I was all soaked with blood issuing from
the man's side after he had sent forth his spirit . . . I
saw the God of hosts violently racked. Darkness with
its clouds had covered the corpse of the Ruler; a gloom,
murky beneath the clouds, overwhelmed its pure
splendour.

With the death of Christ it seems that darkness has finally
overcome the light and that evil has triumphed. But not so,
says the cross:

On me the Son of God suffered for a time; for that cause
I now tower up secure in majesty beneath the heavens
and I am enabled to heal everyone who holds me in
awe . . . You see! the Lord of glory, guardian of heaven-
kingdom, then honoured me above the trees of the forest
. . . Now, my beloved man, I enjoin you to declare this
vision to people; make it plain by your words that it is
the tree of glory on which almighty God suffered for the
many sins of mankind and for the old deeds of Adam.

The personalizing of the cross in this poem is a stroke of
imaginative brilliance, allowing the reader to enter into the
reality of Christ's sufferings from a startlingly new perspective. Through the eyes of this poet, the pain and death
endured by Christ is far from involuntary; rather, he
embraces his destiny willingly in the highest tradition of the
heroes of the contemporary pagan epics. Significant also is

the location of Christ's victory in these events. The battle with evil is won at the very moment when evil appears to have triumphed, the cross of death becomes the cross of victory. For this poet, it is not the resurrection which is the point of conquest. It is 'the Lord of victories' who is taken from the cross and laid in the tomb; the resurrection only confirms what has already been achieved.

୧୫୬୬

Francis of Assisi is one of the great saints of Christendom. Born in 1182, the son of a rich fabric merchant and his French wife, in his youth he was spirited, gregarious and fun-loving. His imagination was early captured by the glamour and romantic ideals of the troubadour tradition, and tales of chivalry and the glory of knighthood abounded. Inspired by dreams of daring and valour, Francis enlisted in the local army of Assisi as they went into battle against neighbouring Perugia. His dreams of military glory were soon shattered. Assisi lost the battle and Francis was captured and imprisoned in Perugia, returning home upon his release a year later a sick and disillusioned young man.

In 1204, Francis set out on another attempt to engage in military action. But when he was twenty-five miles from home, a powerful mystical experience caused him to return to Assisi. Once there, the mysterious workings of God within his soul issued forth in a graphic vision of the crucified Christ. This vision was to inspire and direct the rest of his life, and Francis began to seek God more urgently in solitude and prayer.

Francis wrestled and agonized his way through the early life-shattering experiences of his growing faith. As his spiritual sight became clearer, he began to emerge with a vision which was – and still is – one of the greatest gifts and challenges to the institutional church and its members. For Francis' spirituality and way of life embodied nothing more – or less – than a literal living out of the gospel life exemplified by Christ.

Incurring his father's wrath, Francis appropriated some of his wealth and distributed it to the poor. He made a pilgrimage to Rome, where he exchaged his clothes for the filthy rags of a poor beggar. He had always hated and feared leprosy, but under the impulse of the divine love that was driving him he was able to embrace a leper, and found his entire outlook mysteriously changed. In 1206 Francis' father took him to court, furious at what he saw as the cavalier treatment of his goods and wealth. And it was at this point that Francis dramatically stripped himself naked; marking publicly his total renunciation of his father's outlook and his own earlier life. From now on Francis' life was to be dedicated to a loving and life-long service of God alone.

In the years that followed, Francis was joined by others drawn by the challenge, simplicity and attractiveness of his gospel life. His understanding of the Order of Poor Friars, as they came to be known, was not based on the monastic rule of any other order then in existence. The three vows of poverty, chastity and obedience were embraced, simply as expressions of the life of Christ as seen in the Gospels. For the Friars this was worked out in the form of an itinerant life of prayer and preaching, supported by manual work and begging.

As time passed and the Order grew, tensions arose as to the future direction the work should take. Some wanted to move away from the radical and literal gospel simplicity of the earlier days, with the establishing of more settled communities and the accumulating of some possessions. But Francis remained true to his spiritual roots; his whole life and work inspired by the dramatic vision of the crucified Christ he had received so many years before. All that had happened since was an expression of his ever-deepening union with God in Christ. In 1224, as his earthly life drew towards its close, while on Mount La Verna he received the five wounds of the stigmata on his body. Francis' prayer had been that he might be able to enter more fully into the suffering and love of Christ's passion, and he carried the wounds of this passion for the remaining two years of his life. As his death approached, Francis asked to be laid naked on the ground, after the example of Christ who was hung naked on the cross.

In his book *Franciscan Spirituality*,[2] Brother Ramon detects a sense of inevitability in Francis about his long and arduous pilgrimage to La Verna, perhaps echoing that same sense of inevitability as Jesus approached Jerusalem for the final time. His public ministry receded as his whole being was drawn deeper into the silence and mystery that is God. The prayer of Francis on this solitary mountain was the ultimate of self-offering, as he sought to be totally identified with the sufferings of his Saviour:

My Lord Jesus Christ, I pray you to grant me two graces before I die; the first is that during my life I may feel in my soul and in my body, as much as possible, the pain which you, dear Jesus, sustained in the hour of Your most bitter Passion. The second is that I may feel in my heart, as much as possible, that excessive love which You, O Son of God, were inflamed in willingly enduring such suffering for us sinners.[3]

This is redemptive suffering at its most intense. The Christian believer feels called to seek identification with the passion of Christ, not for reasons of masochism, but

because of a burning desire both to suffer with Christ, and
to reach out to a suffering world with his love and compassion. This desire is totally biblical in its foundation:

> I have been crucified with Christ; and it is no longer I
> who live, but it is Christ who lives in me.
>
> *Galatians 2.19b–20*

> Then Jesus told his disciples, 'If any want to become my
> followers, let them deny themselves and take up their
> cross and follow me. For those who want to save their life
> will lose it, and those who lose their life for my sake will
> find it.'
>
> *Matthew 16.24–5*

> I want to know Christ and the power of his resurrection
> and the sharing of his sufferings by becoming like him in
> his death.
>
> *Philippians 3.10*

> I am now rejoicing in my sufferings for your sake.
>
> *Colossians 1.24*

The words we read and the prayers we pray, almost
without thinking sometimes, would cause us to hesitate and
shrink back if we allowed our hearts and souls to be open
to the full weight of their impact. For the message of
Scripture, and of the life of St Francis, is that such costly
and radical openness *is* the way of life and fulfilment. It
fulfils not in the way the world thinks of fulfilment, with its
selfish insistence on what *I* want, and what I consider to
be in *my* best interests; but rather in the way of releas-
ing and letting go, allowing self to be transformed and
fulfilled within the wider reality that is Christ crucified and
risen:

When a man or woman opens his or her heart to God in so dramatic and naked a manner, then they are taken at their word. Francis was willing to pay the price of suffering love, and this is a mark of the believer who has been united with the will and yearning of God. He knew that whatever suffering was involved, there was sheer joy at the end of the road, for it would mean the salvation of his brothers and sisters, and a sharing of the divine compassion that would ultimately reconcile the whole cosmos to God.[4]

Compared with our knowledge of many of the details of the life of Francis, we know comparatively little about the English mystic Julian of Norwich, born nearly 120 years after Francis' death. We know that she was born around 1342, and died almost eighty years later in 1420. We know that for a significant period of her life she lived as an anchoress, or recluse, in a small cell attached to St Julian's church in Norwich. However, we cannot be sure of her identity, as it is likely that Julian took her name from the church with which she was associated, rather than the other way round. We do not know whether she was a religious, living the life of an anchoress with the support of a community behind her, or whether she came to the solitary life as a laywoman. It was not unusual in the Middle Ages for people to seek expression of their religious needs through becoming recluses, rather than in joining one of the recognized religious orders. Norwich alone records fifty such recluses between the thirteenth century and the Reformation. Some have suggested that there are clues in Julian's writings to suggest that in her earlier life, she had been married and had had children.

The full factual details of Julian's life continue to elude us, and we are faced with the paradox of a woman who has come so vividly alive to us through her writings, and yet at the same time, remains an enigma. Apart from a brief reference by her younger contemporary Marjorie Kempe in her own book,[5] and some mention of her in some wills and bequests, all the information we have about Julian comes from her own writing. Julian had prayed that she might come to understand more fully the meaning of Christ's passion, and her book, *Revelations of Divine Love*, tells what evolved in response to that prayer. She begins by describing how her prayers were answered by a serious illness which took her to the point of death, and of a series of sixteen visions she received while in that state. The book exists in two forms, the Short Text and the Long Text. The shorter form is largely restricted to a description of the content of the visions, and is likely to have been written fairly soon after the event. But the longer form, while also detailing the visions, contains much more in the way of commentary and theological reflection, and was probably produced more than twenty years after the original visions.

The heart of Julian's prayer had been an intense desire to understand Christ's passion more fully:

> It seemed to me that I could feel the Passion of Christ to some extent, but yet I longed by God's grace to feel it more strongly. I thought how I wished I had been there with Mary Magdalene and with others who were Christ's dear friends, and therefore I longed to be shown him in the flesh so that I might have more knowledge of our Saviour's bodily suffering and of our Lady's fellow-suffering and that of all his true friends who then saw his pain; I wanted to be one of them and suffer with him . . . I begged for this so that after the showing I would have a truer perception of Christ's Passion.[6]

God took Julian at her word. Crucifixion is a horrific experience, involving exposure, loss of blood and suffocation over an agonizingly drawn-out period of time. What followed for Julian was a vision of Christ's crucifixion and an experience of his sufferings in raw and unmitigated detail:

> At the time when our Lord and blessed Saviour was dying on the cross it seemed to me that there was a bitter, dry wind and it was wonderfully cold; and it was shown that while all the precious blood that could bleed from the dear body had done so, there yet remained some moisture in Christ's dear flesh. Loss of blood and pain drying him from within, and blasts of wind and cold coming from without, met together in the dear body of Christ . . . And though this pain was bitter and sharp, it seemed to me that it lasted a very long time, and painfully dried up all the vitality of Christ's flesh. So I saw Christ's dear flesh dying, seemingly bit by bit, drying up with amazing agony. And as long as there was any vital spirit in Christ's flesh, so long did he suffer pain. This long agony made it seem to me that he had been dead for a full week – dying, on the point of passing away, suffering the final throes of death.[7]

This kind of contemplation is hard for us to grasp today, and we may be tempted to suspect that a morbid or hysterical personality lies behind the desire for such an experience. But Julian's desire does not stem from a self-centred masochism, and we do not find in her writing any urgency to acquire intense religious experiences simply for their own sake. She does not start, as most of us tend to do, with herself. Rather than have Christ share her experience, she seeks instead to enter into his, which is something completely different. Julian is enabled to accompany Christ each step of the way on his crucifixion journey, and she believes she knows how this journey is bound to end. She saw

> the cruel pain that he suffered, which we should consider with contrition and compassion; at this time our Lord revealed that to me, and gave me the power and grace to see it. And I watched for the last breath with all my might, and expected to see the body completely dead.[8]

But at the very climax of events, at that point when it seems there can only be one conclusion, the utterly unexpected happens, startles Julian and almost takes our breath away:

> But I did not see him like that. And just at the very moment when it seemed to me that . . . his life could last no longer and the end must be revealed, suddenly I saw, while looking at the same cross, that his blessed expression changed. The changing of his blessed expression changed mine, and I was as glad and as happy as it was possible to be. Then our Lord made me think happily, 'Where is there now one jot of your pain or your sorrow?' And I was very happy.[9]

The outcome is totally unexpected, and catches us off-guard. In an instant, death is transformed into life, and sadness into joy. We are more used to finding sorrow in the crucifixion, and joy beyond it in the resurrection. But here, through Julian's vision, we are challenged to see joy *in the crucifixion itself*. We saw earlier that *The Dream of the Rood*, five centuries before, expressed a similar idea, where the crucifixion itself is seen as the victorious event, which the resurrection simply confirms. And this is not all. In facing the sufferings of Christ head on, without flinching, Julian finds that the meaning of life in general, and of her own sufferings in particular, attain their proper perspective and place. As part of the first revelation, Julian has been given a glimpse of the purpose of all the visions:

> Our Lord showed me a spiritual vision of his familiar love. I saw that for us he is everything that we find good and comforting. He is our clothing, wrapping us for love, embracing and enclosing us for tender love, so that he can never leave us, being himself everything that is good for us, as I understand it . . . And he has made us only for himself and restored us by his blessed Passion and cares for us with his blessed love. And all this is out of his goodness.[10]

〰️

In 1940, Brother Roger settled alone in the tiny Burgundian village of Taizé. He had no fixed agenda, beyond seeking a closer encounter with God in the solitude of a human wasteland. Being war time, he found himself offering shelter and hiding to political refugees, especially Jews. As time went on, other young men from various Christian denominations joined him, attracted by his simple living out of a gospel life of total commitment to God and loving service of the poor. From the earliest days of the community, small fraternities were set up as loving and prayerful presences in some of the poorest parts of the world.

Compelled by the potency of a truly ecumenical community life and its wholehearted commitment to the world's poor, young adults began spontaneously to visit Taizé in the 1960s, and continue to visit in their thousands every year. Every Friday evening, the highlight of the week's programme consists of prayer around the cross. The icon of the cross is laid upon the floor, and people are encouraged, if they wish, to lay their foreheads on the wood of the cross as they kneel in prayer. But this is no mere veneration of an icon; it is a way of entrusting to God, by a physical prayer of the body, one's own burdens and those of others. It becomes not only an identification with Christ in his passion, but also a way of expressing communion with all those who suffer, have suffered or will suffer, across the world and throughout time.

The Dream of the Rood – St Francis – Julian of Norwich – Taizé; the golden thread continues. The cross, if we pray for the courage to face its challenges, will lead us into uncharted waters; drawing us ever deeper into knowledge of self and union with God and the whole of creation. It offers us a breathtaking journey into the limitless love of God, who alone is the source of all our life and peace.

Ideas for Prayer and Reflection

Most merciful God,
who by the death and resurrection of your Son Jesus
    Christ
delivered and saved the world:
grant that by faith in him who suffered on the cross
we may triumph in the power of his victory;
through Jesus Christ your Son our Lord,
who is alive and reigns with you,
in the unity of the Holy Spirit,
one God, now and for ever.
Amen.

Collect for the Fifth Sunday of Lent, *Common Worship*

The death of someone we love is always shattering. To love is to carry another within oneself, to keep a special place in one's heart for him or her. This spiritual space is nourished by a physical presence; death, then, tears out a part of our own heart. Those who deny the suffering of death have never truly loved; they live in a spiritual illusion.

To celebrate death, then, is not to deny this laceration and the grief it involves, it is to give space to live it, to speak about it, and even to sing of it. It is to give mutual support, looking the reality in the face and placing all in the heart of God in deep trust. Jesus did not come to abolish suffering and death, but he showed us the way to live them both fruitfully. We must penetrate the mystery of suffering by surrender and sacrifice.

Jean Vanier[11]

And now we give you thanks
because, for our salvation,
he was obedient even to death on the cross.
The tree of shame was made the tree of glory;
and where life was lost, there life has been restored.

Short Eucharistic Preface
Fifth Sunday of Lent to the Wednesday of Holy Week,
Common Worship

Mountain Ash

It can be seen above the bank of the river,
On the edge
of bog and wind,
its earth a crack in the sheer rock.

A pale trunk
with a cross-piece
bare and bent,
the same grace as the wood of the Cross.

Branches, arms, twigs,
pocked
with bruises,
rough, rude, like Christ's ribs.

And blood in drops on the tree
on the edge
of bog and wind
will spread from the growth of God's mercy.

Euros Bowen[12]

✧

The cross is the abyss of wonders, the centre of desires, the school of virtues, the house of wisdom, the throne of love, the theatre of joys, and the place of sorrows. It is the root of happiness, and the gate of heaven . . .

The only reason why this glorious object is so publicly admired by churches and kingdoms . . . is because it is truly the most glorious. It is the root of comforts and the fountain of joys. It is the only supreme and sovereign spectacle in all worlds. It is a well of life beneath in which we may see the face of heaven above, and the only mirror wherein all things appear in their proper colours: that is, sprinkled with the blood of our Lord and Saviour. The cross of Christ is the Jacob's ladder by which we ascend into the highest heavens.

Thomas Traherne, *Centuries of Meditations*

✧

Eternal Light, shine into our hearts.
Eternal Goodness, deliver us from evil.
Eternal Power, be our support.
Eternal Darkness, scatter the darkness of ignorance.
Eternal Pity, have mercy upon us.
And the blessing of God Almighty, the Father, the Son
    and the Holy Spirit,
be with us and remain with us, this day and always.
Amen.

St Alcuin[13]

Notes

Act 1 Advent

Scene 1 Seasons of Darkness: Advent

1 Maria Boulding, *The Coming of God*, SPCK, 1982; re-issued Canterbury Press, 2001.
2 While this is still the majority view, the general assumption of the pagan origins of Christmas has been challenged in recent years. See T. J. Talley, *The Origins of the Liturgical Year*, Pueblo Publishing Company Inc., 1986, pp. 87ff. I am grateful to Bishop Kenneth Stevenson for drawing my attention to this material.
3 Immanuel Velikovsky, *Ages in Chaos, III: Ramses II and His Time*, Sidgwick & Jackson, 1978.

Scene 2 Darkness: The Place of Revelation

1 W. Blake, 'To Nobodaddy' in *The Complete Poems*, Penguin, 1977, p. 144.
2 C. S. Lewis, *The Problem of Pain*, Fount, 1940, p. 81.
3 Raymond Lull, *The Tree of Love*, Part II, ch.1, 8. Quoted in Patrick Grant, *A Dazzling Darkness: An Anthology of Western Mysticism*, Fount, 1985.

Scene 3 Darkness: The Womb of Life

1 J. P. Newell, *The Book of Creation: An Introduction to Celtic Spirituality*, Canterbury Press, 1999, pp. 3–4. I am indebted to Dr Newell's work for many of the ideas in this section of the chapter, and for his warm encouragement of my general explorations in Celtic Spirituality.

2 John Scotus Eriugena, *Periphyseon (The Division of Nature)*, Bellarmin, 1987, 749D.

3 *Periphyseon*, 697B.

4 A. J. Scott, 'A Lecture on History', *The Manchester Examiner*, 2 October 1847; cited in Newell, *The Book of Creation*, p. 6.

5 *Periphyseon*, 773C.

6 Newell, *The Book of Creation*, p. 4.

7 C. J. Moore (ed.), *A. Carmichael, Carmina Gadelica: Hymns and Incantations*, Floris Books, 1994, no. 252.

8 Henry Vaughan, 'The Night' in H. Gardner (ed.), *The New Oxford Book of English Verse*, Oxford University Press, 1972, p. 347. I am grateful to the Revd David Scott for drawing my attention to this poem in the context of 'creative darkness'.

9 Henry Vaughan, in *The New Oxford Book of English Verse*, p. 348.

10 Thomas Traherne, *Centuries of Meditation*, IV, 77. Cited in P. Grant, *A Dazzling Darkness*, Fount, 1985, pp. 85–6.

Scene 4 Darkness and Dreaming

1 Laurens van der Post, 'The Time and the Space', *Jung and the Story of Our Time*, Penguin, 1978.

2 Russ Parker, *Healing Dreams: Their Power and Purpose in your Spiritual Life*, SPCK, 1988. I am indebted to this book for some of the thoughts and ideas in this chapter.

3 A person suffering from manic depression was not aware of dreaming at all. When moving into a period of sustained equilibrium however, he began to experience a conscious dreaming process for the first time. It is possible that the chemical imbalance found in such illnesses as manic depression somehow interferes with the normal dreaming process, and that this in turn exacerbates the symptoms of the illness.

4 Robert Bly, *A Little Book on the Human Shadow*, Element, 1992.

5 *A Little Book on the Human Shadow*, pp. 17ff.

6 *A Little Book on the Human Shadow*, p. 18.

7 *Jung and the Story of Our Time*, p. 9.

8 *Jung and the Story of Our Time*, p. 9.

9 'The Time and the Space', *Jung and the Story of Our Time*, p. 10.

10 Laurens van der Post, *The Heart of the Hunter*, Penguin, 1965.

Act 2 *Lent*

Scene 1 *Seasons of Darkness: Lent*

1 *The Origins of the Liturgical Year*, p. 191.
2 Harry Williams, *The True Wilderness*, Fontana, 1976, p. 28.
3 *The True Wilderness*, p. 30.
4 *The True Wilderness*, pp. 31–2.
5 Winston S. Churchill, *Thoughts and Adventures* (1932), Odhams Press, 1947, p. 219.
6 Quoted in Laurens van der Post, *Feather Fall*, Penguin, 1995, pp. 88–9.
7 Maria Boulding, *The Coming of God*, SPCK, 1982, repr. Canterbury Press, 2001, pp. 35–6.
8 Janet Morley, *All Desires Known*, SPCK, 1992, p. 80.

Scene 2 *Darkness and Being Alone*

1 Thomas Merton, *Seeds of Contemplation*, Anthony Clarke, 1972, p. 62.
2 Beverly Lancour Sinke, *Wrestling with God and Cancer*, Twenty-Third Publications/Bayard, 2000.
3 J. F. Webb (trans.), 'Bede: Life of Cuthbert' in *The Age of Bede*, Penguin, 1965, pp. 65–6. Permission sought.
4 'Bede: Life of Cuthbert' in *The Age of Bede*, p. 75.
5 *Seeds of Contemplation*, p. 62.
6 Jean Vanier, *Community and Growth*, Darton, Longman & Todd, 1979 , pp. 329–30.

Scene 3 *Darkness and Unknowing*

1 Helen Waddell (trans.), *The Desert Fathers*, Vintage Spiritual Classics, 1998, p. 27.
2 Abraham J. Malherbe and Everett Ferguson (trans.), *Gregory of Nyssa: The Life of Moses*, Paulist Press, 1978, p. 95.
3 *Gregory of Nyssa: The Life of Moses*, p. 95.
4 Melvyn Matthews, *Both Alike to Thee: The Retrieval of the Mystical Way*, SPCK, 2000.
5 *Both Alike to Thee*, p. 1.
6 Thomas Merton, *Contemplative Prayer*, Darton, Longman & Todd, 1973, p. 26.

7 *Both Alike to Thee*, p. 4.

8 Brian Keenan, *An Evil Cradling*, Vintage, 1992, p. 230.

9 Ruth Burrows, *Before the Living God*, Sheed & Ward, 1975.

10 *The Cloud of Unknowing*, p. 252.

11 Janet Morley, *All Desires Known*, SPCK, 1992, p. 84.

Scene 4 Darkness and Disability

1 Joni Eareckson and Joe Mosser, *Joni*, Zondervan, 1978, p. 7.

2 *Joni*, pp. 178, 206.

3 C. S. Lewis, *The Problem of Pain*, Fount, 1940, p. 81.

4 From an unpublished paper, 'How to make Manic Depression work for you'. Quoted with permission.

5 Quoted in Donald Grout, *A History of Western Music*, J. M. Dent & Sons, 1962, p. 524.

6 *A History of Western Music*, p. 524.

7 John Hull, *In the Beginning there was Darkness*, SCM Press, 2001, p. 48.

8 Janet Morley, *All Desires Known*, SPCK, 1992, p. 13.

9 John Hull, *On Sight and Insight*, OneWorld, 1997.

Scene 5 Darkness and Suffering

1 I am indebted to Anthony Phillips for many of the ideas in this section. See chapter 3, 'The Absent God' in his *God B.C.*, Oxford University Press, 1977, pp. 51–72.

2 Elizabeth Spearing, *Julian of Norwich: Revelations of Divine Love*, Penguin, 1998, ch. 27, p. 80

3 Sheila Upjohn, *Why Julian Now?*, Darton, Longman & Todd, 1997, p. 4.

4 Mstslav Rostropovitch, from an interview in *The Times*, 27 March 2002.

5 Rowan Williams, *Writing in the Dust: Reflections on 11th September and its Aftermath*, Hodder & Stoughton, 2002.

6 *Writing in the Dust*, p. 2.

7 *Writing in the Dust*, pp. x–xi.

8 Quoted in Brendan O'Malley, *God at Every Gate*, Canterbury Press, 1997, p. 112.

9 *Writing in the Dust*, pp. 75–6.

10 Jean Vanier, *The Broken Body*, Darton, Longman & Todd, 1988.

11 *Writing in the Dust*, pp. 77–8.
12 Brendan O'Malley, *God at Every Gate*, p. 113.

Scene 6 Darkness: Passion and Death

1 S. A. J. Bradley (trans.), *Anglo-Saxon Poetry*, J. M. Dent, 1995, pp. 158–63.
2 Brother Ramon SSF, *Franciscan Spirituality*, SPCK, 1994, pp. 178–9.
3 *Franciscan Spirituality*, p. 180, quoting *Fior Consideration 3 (Omn 1448)*.
4 *Franciscan Spirituality*, p. 181.
5 B. A. Windeatt, *The Book of Marjorie Kempe*, Penguin, 1985, ch. 18, pp. 77–8.
6 Elizabeth Spearing, *Julian of Norwich: Revelations of Divine Love*, Penguin, 1998, ch. 2, pp. 42–3.
7 *Revelations of Divine Love*, ch. 16, p. 65.
8 *Revelations of Divine Love*, ch. 21, p. 71.
9 *Revelations of Divine Love*, ch. 21, p. 71.
10 *Revelations of Divine Love*, ch. 5, pp. 47–8.
11 Jean Vanier, *Man and Woman He Made Them*, Darton, Longman & Todd, 1988.
12 Euros Bowen, *Poems*, Gwasg Gomer, 1974, p. 43.
13 Quoted in this form in *Celebrating Common Prayer: Pocket Version*, Mowbray, 1994, p. 246. Permission sought.